Editing

FilmCraft

Editing

Justin Chang

ILEX

First published in the UK in 2012 by
I L E X
210 High Street
Lewes
East Sussex BN7 2NS
www.ilex-press.com
Copyright © 2012 The Ilex Press Limited

Publisher: Alastair Campbell
Creative Director: Peter Bridgewater
Associate Publisher: Adam Juniper
Managing Editors: Natalia Price-Cabrera & Zara Larcombe
Editor: Tara Gallagher
Art Director: James Hollywell
In-house Designer: Kate Haynes
Designer: Grade Design
Picture Manager: Katie Greenwood
Colour Origination: Ivy Press Reprographics

British Library Cataloguing-in-Publication Data
A catalogue record for this book is available from
the British Library.

ISBN: 978-1-907579-56-1

Special thanks to Caroline Bailey, Dave Kent, Darren Thomas, Phil
Moad and Cheryl Thomas at The Kobal Collection, for all of their
effort and support.

Every effort has been made to acknowledge pictures. However,
the publisher apologises if there are any unintentional omissions.

Printed and bound in China
10 9 8 7 6 5 4 3 2

Introduction

It is a well-known axiom that editing is the only cinematic discipline that did not precede the cinema itself. For centuries, writers, directors, actors, dancers, composers and production designers had a natural outlet for their talents in the theater, while still photography existed long before the key innovation of movement that gave rise to cinema. Even then, the act of filming required merely a camera and an object of the camera's attention. But the act of filmmaking suddenly required an editor, a creative technician who could step in after the performance had been captured and complete the illusion by arranging it into a form worthy of projection.

Editing is not only unique to cinema but a uniquely difficult discipline to comprehend, let alone discuss—a state of affairs to which this book is intended as some small corrective. Yet even some of the film editors interviewed here have difficulty articulating the precise nature of their work and the strategies they apply in the cutting room. "I can't explain how I do what I do," Michael Kahn admits, while Anne V. Coates offers, "I just cut the way I feel." One has only to witness the famous match cut from **Lawrence of Arabia** (1962) or the D-Day sequence that opens **Saving Private Ryan** (1998), to single out but two examples from these remarkable careers, to know that on the level that matters most, they know exactly what they're doing.

For more concrete language on the subject, both Kahn and Coates directed me to their colleague Walter Murch, who has done more than anyone else inside or outside his profession to illuminate the public understanding of his discipline. Murch has described film editing as synonymous with film construction—the careful assembly of a motion picture, scene by scene, shot by shot, frame by frame. Yet in his book *In the Blink of an Eye*, he also addresses a seemingly contradictory idea, which is the old adage that film editing is just "where you cut out the bad bits." And he concedes that this shopworn notion, annoyingly reductive though it may be, nonetheless holds a kernel of truth.

Editing, after all, is an art achieved largely by subtraction, by a negation of those elements that do not serve the final product. Assembly, one of the most frequently used terms in the editor's lexicon, can only take place after a significant amount of disassembly. Whatever tools the editor may be using, it is his or her job to comb through the footage, isolate the desired elements, and arrange them into a coherent and entertaining shape. More often than not, that shape is determined as much by what is taken out as by what is left in.

In any given film, then, the actors may impress us with the intensity and focus of their performances, and the cinematography may dazzle us with its sweep and beauty, but it is the film editor who maximizes the impact of these elements, sometimes by limiting rather than extending their duration. It is the film editor who, by dropping a few frames, can make the crucial difference between a joke that kills and one that overstays its welcome. Everything you see in a film is there because the editor decided to show it to you, and you can be assured that there is plenty more that the editor opted to withhold.

Thus, even the finest editing job, however elegant or economical, may be impossible to fully appreciate unless the viewer has seen the raw materials and thus has some sense of what has been discarded in the first place. As you read this book, from time to time you may catch a glimpse of those unseen, unheard moments: the snippets of song that Virginia Katz had to leave on the cutting-room floor of **Dreamgirls** (2006), the hilarious Robin Williams scene that Lee Smith saw scrapped from **Dead Poets Society** (1989), the extended Mexican wedding sequence that Stephen Mirrione ended up trimming for **Babel** (2006), or the lengthy dialogue passages that Valdís Óskarsdóttir had to excise, to her anguish, from **Julien Donkey-Boy** (1999).

This book is not a technical treatise but a series of conversations (from which my own voice has been excised) with 17 of the world's leading practitioners of film editing, sharing their personal and professional insights into the movies they've cut, the directors they've collaborated with and the ever-changing nature of their specific medium. While the bulk of the interviews were conducted with editors based in the US, they also include contributions from Asia and Europe, hopefully providing a counter-perspective on the dominant mode of editing practiced within the Hollywood studio system. And just as a film editor may construct a picture with an eye toward establishing echoes, parallels and contrapuntal rhythms between individual scenes, so these chapters were assembled with the hope of placing these contributors in conversation with one another, creating an implicit dialogue between their respective views and methodologies.

It is delightful, if not downright perverse, to imagine a direct conversation between Walter Murch, with his precise hierarchy of priorities of when and where to cut based on the emotional effect and visual continuity of a scene, and William Chang Suk-ping, for whom the joy of editing lies in his ability to flout every rule and convention in pursuit of a restless cinematic poetry. Certainly the two of them would disagree on the advisability of having an editor present on set: Chang, who typically serves as both production designer and editor on the same film, sees these dual duties as a way of informing the total look of a film, whereas Murch considers the editor as a stand-in for the audience and rigorously avoids visiting the set whenever possible, so as to ensure that his first impressions will come from the dailies alone.

It would be similarly instructive to draw comparisons between the work of Christopher Rouse, who structures the action movies of Paul Greengrass in hyperkinetic fragments, and that of the Taiwanese editor Liao Ching-sung, whose assembly on Hou Hsiao-hsien's **Flowers of Shanghai** (1998) contains fewer cuts in its entirety than any five minutes of **The Bourne Ultimatum** (2007). That pulse-quickening action picture won Rouse the Academy Award for best editing, a significant institutional endorsement of a cutting-edge style, so to speak, that has admirers and detractors alike.

If Rouse's and Greengrass's style seems emblematic of an overall, arguably generational shift toward ever more rapid cutting in modern cinema, so does another film that recently won the Oscar for best editing: David Fincher's **The Social Network** (2010), the architecture of which is discussed here at some length by Fincher's editors, Angus Wall and Kirk Baxter. Together with Fincher, Baxter and Wall are also at the fore of an even more pervasive trend: the industry's seemingly inexorable shift toward the digitization of filmmaking across the board. It's a transformation that has already swept through cutting rooms the world over, where flatbed machines like the KEM and the Steenbeck have long been replaced by non-linear systems such as Avid and Final Cut Pro.

Many of the editors interviewed here, among them Anne Voase Coates, Joel Cox, Hervé de Luze, Tim Squyres and Dylan Tichenor, first learned how to cut on film, and several of them concede that they would not have survived and thrived had they not gone with the electronic flow—a transition that some of their less remembered colleagues were not willing to make. As Richard Marks opines, "If you aren't willing to change, you shouldn't be editing." Still, no less an editorial giant than Michael Kahn managed to hold out for longer than any of his contemporaries; only this past year, when editing Steven Spielberg's **The Adventures of Tintin: The Secret of the Unicorn** (2011) and **War Horse** (2011), did Kahn switch to an Avid, setting his Moviola aside.

Both Kahn and Dylan Tichenor observe that among less experienced editors, digital editing—with its ability to store infinite versions of a scene and thus eliminate the fear of making "the wrong cut"—may encourage a certain mindlessness in post-production, a lack of focus and forethought that would never have been tolerated in the days of editing on film. They →

are not wrong. Nor would they necessarily disagree with their fellow contributors here that in the right hands, the non-linear system can be a powerful, even indispensable tool.

But a tool it remains and no less than the hot splicers once used by editors such as the late Dede Allen, the digital apparatus requires a skilled, focused editor at the helm in order to maximize its efficiency. This is the glory of film editing: Final Cut Pro may have rendered trim bins and grease pencils obsolete, but it has no more eliminated the need for an editor than Microsoft Word has eliminated the need for a writer. As every editor interviewed here will tell you, their work requires a hundred creative decisions each day that a computer can merely enable them to make. These decisions directly involve not merely rhythm and tempo, music and sound, but also the quality and range of a performance, and thus the emotional content of the entire film.

One of the most important decisions the editor can make concerns the degree to which his or her hand will be visible to the viewer. It is worth bearing in mind that every cut, whether it is intended to heighten the reality of a moment or point out its artificiality, represents a disruption, a rip in the film's fabric, and perhaps the cinema's most irrational gesture. As Murch notes in *In the Blink of an Eye*, "The instantaneous displacement achieved by the cut is not anything that we experience in ordinary life"—a more reasoned phrasing of Jean-Luc Godard's famous maxim that "Cinema is truth 24 times a second, and every cut is a lie."

Viewed through this prism, it took only six years for the purity of the Lumière Brothers' single-shot **Arrival of a Train at La Ciotat** (1896) to be corrupted by the influence of cross-cutting in Edwin S. Porter's **The Great Train Robbery** (1903), and in the many years since those twin railway-themed milestones, audiences have long become inured to the cut as a staple of cinematic grammar. It may represent a lie, but a century's worth of cinema shows that it is capable of enabling a deeper kind of truth.

The rules of traditional Hollywood filmmaking exalt editing that is seamless to the point of invisibility, deepening the viewer's immersion in the story without calling attention to itself. Joel Cox, who has edited nearly 30 films in this vein for Clint Eastwood, is one of the staunchest proponents of this classical method. For him, a great cut is "a cut you didn't see," and indeed, the slow, devastating accrual of emotions in pictures like **Million Dollar Baby** (2004) and **Letters from Iwo Jima** (2006) requires a subdued touch, a willingness to let images breathe and speak for themselves.

And yet there is no shortage of editors who break this rule all the time, superbly: One thinks of Lee Smith, juxtaposing multiple lines of action in **The Dark Knight** (2008) and **Inception** (2010); or Stephen Mirrione, in **21 Grams** (2003) and **Babel**, spanning time as well as space in a single cut; Valdís Óskarsdóttir, dodging in and out of Jim Carrey's consciousness in **Eternal Sunshine of the Spotless Mind** (2004); or Richard Marks, who spent months perfecting those long, luxuriant dissolves between past and present in **The Godfather: Part II** (1974). One is never unconscious of the editing when watching these films, and yet awareness is no hindrance to engaging with the stories they're telling.

And as Tim Squyres observes, editing is the rare job in filmmaking "where you're involved in telling the whole story," nailing one of the few ideas that perhaps every person interviewed here can agree upon. Indeed, these 17 editors were chosen because of their unusually deep investment in the art of storytelling, and their concern for the quality of any film that bears their name. This commitment is apparent not only in the discrimination with which they choose their projects, but also their willingness to follow their directors wherever they go, sometimes at the risk of foregoing greater commercial success.

One should never assume that this is universally the case. As Hervé de Luze points out, while editors and directors are all but joined at the hip in France, Hollywood does not always command the same loyalty or the same longevity of collaboration. The 17 editors you will meet here are happy exceptions to the rule, and it is with no small measure of awe that I thank them for entrusting me with their own stories, and for giving so generously of their expertise and time.

I am also enormously grateful to the many who made this book possible, not least my own editor, Mike Goodridge, for entrusting me with this project on a tight deadline and showing endless patience with my questions, concerns, and the occasional late copy. Deep thanks and appreciation as well to Zara Larcombe, Natalia Price-Cabrera, and Tara Gallagher of Ilex Press for their enthusiasm and commitment to the FilmCraft series; to Katie Greenwood and the Ivy Group team for providing me access to the invaluable Kobal Collection image archives; and to Jenni McCormick for her incredible generosity on behalf of the American Film Editors.

I am grateful to all my colleagues at *Variety* for putting up with my unusually mercurial work schedule over the past few months. In particular, my warmest thanks to Timothy Gray, for being ever supportive and understanding during a stressful time, and Peter Debruge, for being a reliable and receptive sounding board for the numerous ideas and possibilities that shaped this book.

I would not have been able to secure the participation of my 17 contributors without the kind assistance of Jennifer Chamberlain, Arvin Chen, Hillary Corinne Cook, Chris Day, Harlan Gulko, Paul Hook, Michael Leow, Michael Kupferberg, Jordan Mintzer, Larry Mirisch, Nikolas Palchikoff, David Pollack, Michelle Rasic, Mike Rau, Jeff Sanderson, Brian Skouras, Ariana Swan, Kari Tejerian, Ryan Tracey and Chrissy Woo.

I will never be able to properly express my gratitude to my friend Eugene Suen for giving so generously of his time and knowledge to serve the needs of this project. In addition to conducting, translating and transcribing the interview with Liao Ching-sung, Eugene helped put me in touch with both Mr. Liao and William

Chang Suk-ping, whose presence in this book is a special source of satisfaction and pride.

Thank you to my mother, for your love and support in all things great and small, not least your steadfast conviction that your children need not conform to narrow and unimaginative pathways in life. Thank you to my sister, Stephanie, for always looking out for me, and for teaching me not only to pursue my passions, but to temper them with an ever-deeper knowledge and understanding of the world.

To my amazing girlfriend, Lameese, who has given especially generously of her time, energy and boundless patience during these difficult past few months: In walking alongside me you have comforted, delighted and replenished me when I needed it most. If you are reading this, it means you can have me back now.

Justin Chang

Walter Murch

"I love working with other people and sometimes achieving that miraculous collision of ideas, which makes the finished film something greater than the sum of its parts."

Born in 1943 in New York City, Walter Murch is widely recognized as one of the leading authorities in the field of film editing, as well as one of the few editors equally active in both picture and sound. A graduate of the University of Southern California's School of Cinema-Television, he received his early sound credits mixing and sound-supervising Francis Ford Coppola's **The Rain People** (1969) and **The Godfather** (1972), and George Lucas' **THX 1138** (1971) and **American Graffiti** (1973), before picture-editing his first feature, Coppola's **The Conversation** (1974), which he also sound-designed and mixed. He also wore dual hats on Coppola's **Apocalypse Now** (1979), for which he and his collaborators devised the now-standard 5.1 sound format.

Murch has edited picture and mixed sound on films including Coppola's **The Godfather: Part III** (1990), **Youth Without Youth** (2007) and **Tetro** (2009); Jerry Zucker's **Ghost** (1990) and **First Knight** (1995); Anthony Minghella's **The English Patient** (1996), **The Talented Mr. Ripley** (1999) and **Cold Mountain** (2003); Kathryn Bigelow's **K-19: The Widowmaker** (2002); and Sam Mendes' **Jarhead** (2005). He has been nominated for nine Academy Awards and won three, for best sound on **Apocalypse Now**, and best sound and best film editing on **The English Patient**. Murch's contributions to film reconstruction include 2001's **Apocalypse Now Redux** and the 1998 re-edit of Orson Welles' **Touch of Evil**. He is the director and co-writer of **Return to Oz** (1985).

Walter Murch

The wonderful thing about film construction is that it's such a new thing in the human experience. We've been doing this for barely a hundred years, and we're only just beginning to unlock the possibilities. One of the key discoveries we've made is that the audience can take in more information, faster. We're always pushing the limits of that perceptual envelope, whether it's through complicated visual effects, dense soundtracks or fast cutting.

But I do think there is a limit. If an orchestra is playing Beethoven's Fifth faster than the mind can grasp, it just becomes noise, and that's certainly true visually as well. On the other hand, you can't play it too slow, either. You can't give an audience just one thing to think about. Imagine if all the instruments of an orchestra played the same melody at the same time in the same register—it would be like one big harmonica, boring and not worth the effort. What's interesting instead is when you hear the violins doing something different to the flutes, which are doing something different to the cellos: harmonic interaction.

My rule of thumb is generally to not present more than two-and-a-half thematic layers to the audience at any moment, because I'm interested in the balance between clarity on the one hand and density on the other. If you shove four simultaneous layers at an audience it just becomes a spectacle; they'll catch one or two things, but they won't enjoy the harmonic integration of all the elements, and the number of layers that seems optimal for this is two and a half. In other words: two full layers and another layer coming in or going out, all of this shifting every ten or 15 seconds. Ideally, it is like a good shell game where the audience is kept guessing about where the pea is.

While the pace of editing has generally become faster over the decades, the average number of cuts per minute in **The Birth of a Nation** (1915) is exactly the same as in **Tetro** (2009), made almost a hundred years later: on average, one cut every five-and-a-half seconds. Dziga Vertov's **Man With a Movie Camera**, made in 1929, has a section with the fastest cutting I've ever seen; it's a Cuisinart of frames going by. But the level of apparent density is also determined by how the information is being presented to you. **His Girl Friday** (1940) doesn't have many cuts per minute, but the audience is fire-hosed with rapid dialogue and just barely able to keep up; if Hawks had added fast cutting on top of that, it would have been overwhelming. However, David Fincher in **The Social Network** (2010) combines rapid cutting with rapid dialogue. What I'm saying is that this style comes and goes: counterbalancing Vertov's **Man With a Movie Camera** is Sokurov's **Russian Ark** (2002), which has no cuts at all, something that was only made possible with the arrival of digital cameras and massive hard-drive storage. But over time the trend is generally for faster cutting.

It was one of those happy accidents that I started working in features when technology had progressed, thanks to transistors, to the point where there was no reason the sound editor of a film couldn't also mix it—kind of the sound equivalent of the director of photography also being the camera operator. Right after I'd done **The Godfather** (1972) and **American Graffiti** (1973), Francis' next film was **The Conversation** (1974). "This is a film about sound," he said. "You're a sound person, and you've edited documentaries, so why don't you edit the picture as well?" I thought, great! While it was another notch up in responsibility, it fit the general feeling we had at Zoetrope that the technology, though primitive by today's standards, had reached the point where one person could take on these different roles. It's something I've continued doing for the last 40 years.

Digital technology has only accelerated this merging. In Final Cut Pro, you can have 99 soundtracks with 24 outputs, and so you are almost obliged to take advantage of that resource. The multi-track sound we now create as we edit picture is more complex than the finished soundtracks of some films from the 1950s. And today's editing machines—Avid, Final Cut Pro—allow us to have control of sound levels, equalization, reverb, etc. The technology →

THE CONVERSATION

The first film Walter Murch picture-edited was Francis Ford Coppola's **The Conversation**, which blended a psychological study of an intensely private individual, Harry Caul (Gene Hackman), with a murder-mystery. "Neither of those themes was complete unto itself—by design," Murch says. "Getting those two elements to balance was very tricky. It was not an obvious film construction from the beginning, and there were many screenings where we had to ask, 'What is this film?'"

APOCALYPSE NOW

Murch was the last editor hired to work on this iconic film, joining fellow editors Richard Marks, Jerry Greenberg and Dennis Jakob. Coppola asked Murch to edit the first part of the film, on the principle that the film should turn increasingly strange as it progressed, and Murch, as the newest addition to the team, was theoretically the sanest. "The irony is that the beginning is arguably the craziest section of the film," Murch says.

Indeed, the film's famous opening sequence is an intricate, slow-moving series of hallucinatory dissolves, conjuring nightmarish images of napalm explosions in the Vietnam jungle while also introducing the tormented dreamer, Capt. Willard (Martin Sheen), in his Saigon hotel room. No less intricate than the weave of overlapping images is Murch's soundscape, blurring the whir of chopper blades with the whir of a ceiling fan, while the Doors' "The End" underscores the sense of total immersion in a war- and alcohol-induced haze.

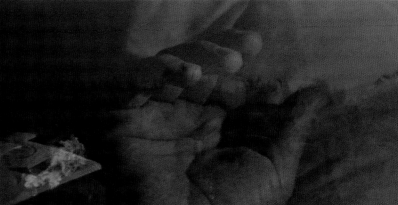

The rule of six

When should you cut? Few editors have put as much rigorous thought into answering that question as Murch, who has compiled a hierarchy of priorities for when and where to transition from one shot to the next. As Murch writes in his book *In the Blink of an Eye*: "The ideal cut (for me) is one that satisfies all the following six criteria at once:

1. it is true to the emotion of the moment
2. it advances the story
3. it occurs at a moment that is rhythmically interesting and "right"
4. it acknowledges what you might call "eye-trace" —the concern with the location and movement of the audience's focus of interest within the frame
5. it respects "planarity"—the grammar of three dimensions transposed by photography to two (the questions of stage-line, etc.)
6. and it respects the three-dimensional continuity of the actual space (where people are in the room and in relation to one another)."

APOCALYPSE NOW

The early footage of Willard experiencing a trauma-induced psychotic episode was filmed as a getting-into-character exercise for Sheen and was never originally intended to be in the finished film. But Coppola found the material too compelling to discard, and Murch found a way to accommodate it into the film's opening sequence—just one example of the many ways in which the writing of **Apocalypse Now** continued well into the post-production phase.

Early drafts of John Milius and Coppola's script had made use of voiceover narration, an idea Coppola had initially discarded. But in August 1977, with a December deadline looming, Murch needed a way to structure the difficult opening scenes and recorded some of the voiceover himself from the original script. War correspondent Michael Herr was brought in to write fresh narration, and his own battle-scarred voice turned out to be an ideal match for Willard's.

encourages this merging of disciplines, which was the original dream of Zoetrope Studios back in 1969.

The Conversation was challenging because it was the first feature I edited, and also the first time I'd used an eight-plate KEM editing machine—I'd worked on Moviolas and Steenbecks before that. And **The Conversation** was a spare, but thematically, complicated picture. Francis' goal for the film was to blend a murder mystery with a character study: Hitchcock meets Hermann Hesse. Yet neither of those themes was complete unto itself—by design. Francis wrote a screenplay where these two themes leant against each other, so that the

leaning itself provided the dynamic structure of the film. We simply didn't have the material to make it either purely a murder-mystery or a character study. Getting those two elements to balance was very tricky, but it was a lovely challenge.

Production had to stop with ten days of shooting left to do. Francis asked Richard Chew and me to put the film together the best way we could, and then we'd see what was missing—at which point we would go to Paramount and ask for a couple of days shooting to fill the gaps. In the end, we restructured the film so that we only needed one extra shot. In the original script Meredith seduces Harry to steal the plans for

his microphones, but in the finished film she steals the tapes that he recorded, folding her into the main storyline and making the problem of the un-shot days evaporate. To clarify this plot twist we had to shoot an over-the-shoulder of Harry pulling a reel off the recorder and finding that it was empty. We did this at Paramount Studios in L.A. in late 1973, building a corner of Harry's workshop on the set of **Chinatown** (1974), and borrowing John Alonzo's camera to shoot it with. If we had kept the camera running, the shot could have panned from Gene Hackman as Harry Caul to Jack Nicholson as Jake Gittes waiting for us to finish so he could get back to work.

We re-mastered **The Conversation** about ten years ago for DVD. So I had the film up on the Avid 30 years after editing it on the KEM: I was curious to see if I could discover some stylistic signature of the difference between the two machines, but it looked perfectly fine. I don't believe the machine on which you edit adds a telltale flavor. Any differences are more attributable to the sensibility of the director, the editor and the zeitgeist. Digital creation and manipulation of the image itself is another matter—that has clearly changed things, turning the fresco of analogue filmmaking into the oil-painting of digital.

I don't think film students who are now learning how to edit are hurt by the fact that →

"**Apocalypse Now** remains the longest post-production experience of any film I've been involved with."

they may never have worked with physical film. It is a fact, of course, that when you were confronted with the physical reality of 1,250,000 feet of film, as we were on **Apocalypse Now**, you had to strategize carefully about what you were doing. With digital editing there is no weight to the media; but a minute of 35mm workprint and sound weighs a pound. For **Apocalypse Now**, that added up to more than seven tons of film. Yet we also had to be able to reach into that seven-ton mass and extract the one frame, weighing a hundredth of an ounce, that would improve a cut. Editing 35mm workprint was a lot of physical work, like ditch-digging, but very precise at the same time, like watchmaking. I am really glad to have experienced it.

Apocalypse Now remains the longest post-production experience of any film I've been involved with. I was on it for two years, but I was the junior partner; Richie Marks was on it for three. At the same time, we were also creating the 5.1 format at Francis' instigation: he wanted the audience to be surrounded by a swirl of sound and to feel the explosions as well as hear them. And we were also constructing a purpose-built mixing studio—it was the first time a computerized board had been used to mix a film.

I was the last editor to join the picture team on **Apocalypse Now** because I had been in England working on **Julia** (1997) while **Apocalypse** was shooting. Early on, in August of 1977, there was an editorial lunch meeting with Francis, Richie, Jerry Greenberg, Dennis Jakob, and me during which Francis said, "I want **Apocalypse Now** to get crazier and crazier as it goes along, and by definition anyone who has worked on this film for any length of time has gone crazy. Dennis, you're clearly the craziest of all, so I want you to edit the ending, and Walter, you're the sanest because you're the newest, so I want you to edit the beginning." The irony is that the beginning is arguably the craziest section of the movie.

When Francis started shooting **Apocalypse Now** in 1976, no film of comparable heft had dared to tackle Vietnam, which was still an open wound in the American psyche. We all felt the responsibility—Francis, obviously, most of all— to tackle this in the deepest way, which involved journeying into a psychic domain that a straight-ahead war film would have avoided. Each time we screened the film, we could track this crazier-and-crazier arc because we were the ones implementing it. But audience reaction was different, I think because of their in-built expectations about what a war film is. The film seemed more normal to them than it really was, up to a point. But it kept bending and bending, and they would resist the bend until they couldn't anymore. Then they would suddenly realize: this is really strange—thinking that the suddenness was in the film itself rather than in their

APOCALYPSE NOW REDUX
Apocalypse Now Redux "was one of those projects that began as a sapling and turned into an oak," according to Murch, who says the impetus for the film was to restore the French plantation scene for the French DVD. The sequence had to be reconstructed from the original negative, spurring Coppola to see if there were any other scenes worth restoring. Thus began an exhaustive reconstruction process that resulted in **Redux**, a version 50 minutes longer than the original theatrical cut and, per Murch, "a very good indication of the screenplay that Francis had when he first went to the Philippines."

perceptions of it. It's our fault as filmmakers, I guess, that we weren't able to make them follow the bend progressively, but we did the best we could. Audience reactions to **Apocalypse** are different now, just through familiarity.

We tried to redress this to some extent with **Apocalypse Now Redux** (2001), which was one of those projects that began as a sapling and turned into an oak. The original impetus was just to make a DVD for the French market with the French plantation scene added as an extra scene. But that scene didn't exist as a complete lift. In the editing of the original **Apocalypse Now** we had whittled the plantation scene down to just five or six shots dissolved together, and then ultimately cut it out completely. So in 2000 we had to go back to the original negative and reconstruct it from scratch. Then Francis thought, "Well, if we're going to all this trouble, let's see if there are any other scenes that we can add." One thing led to another and **Redux** wound up being around 50 minutes longer than the 1979 original. The result is a very good approximation of the screenplay that Francis had when he first went to the Philippines.

I take two layers of notes on the material I am cutting. The first time, in dailies screening, I'll sit there with my laptop, screen darkened, and take free-association notes on whatever has been shot the day before. Then, later on when I'm getting ready to cut a particular sequence of scenes, I will look at all of those dailies again and take another layer of notes, this time being more analytical in my approach, with time-code attached. The first notes, I'm really just letting it wash over me. That first impression only happens, by definition, once. The closest you're ever going to come to how the audience feels is how you felt the first time you saw the material. So I'm very assiduous in capturing whatever it was I was thinking or feeling when I looked at the material for the first time.

Preserving that first impression is an aspect of what I like to call "seeing around the edge of the frame." If you're there on set, witnessing the birth of this material (which the director, the cinematographer, the art director and the actors obviously are), then when you see a scene, you can remember that it was perhaps raining on the day it was shot, and admire how well-hidden that fact is. Or perhaps, "There was a terrible argument right before we got that shot." Or, "It took us eight hours to get this shot—it is (it had better be!) fantastic." It is very hard to unburden yourself of those layers of mental baggage if you have been on set during filming. But as editor, I believe you have an obligation to be as ignorant of all that as possible, because the audience won't know any of it, either. They won't know—or shouldn't know—what the set actually smelled like, or how a small room was made to look big using an 18mm lens, or whatever the →

THE ENGLISH PATIENT

When editing Anthony Minghella's **The English Patient**, Murch had to reinvent many of the script's shifts between past and present time-frames. "We were always on the search for new aural and visual transitions, because if you're going to go back and forth that many times, the transitions have to be interesting and entertaining," he says. In one of the drama's most adroit transitions, Hana (Juliette Binoche) reads a story to her patient, Count Almásy (Ralph Fiennes), spurring him to recall the time in the desert when Katherine (Kristin Scott Thomas) recited the same story around a campfire.

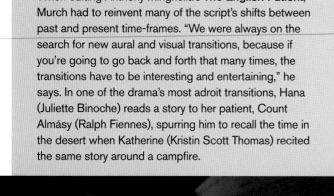

Minghella initially shot a scene for **The English Patient** in which Kip (Naveen Andrews) tells Hana he's ending their relationship. In a prime example of how material intended to serve one dramatic purpose can be reconstituted for another entirely, the scene was scrapped and the footage significantly re-tooled. Andrews was digitally erased from each frame, and shots of Almasy, filmed through the ceiling rafters above, were inserted so as to suggest Hana's point of view as she eavesdrops on his deathbed confession. The resulting scene provided Hana with not only the final puzzle-piece of Almasy's backstory, but also the motivation to aid him in ending his own life.

associations happen to be. The editor is the ombudsman for the audience, and has to put himself in their shoes as much as possible.

The first assembly of **The English Patient** (1996) was four hours and 20 minutes. We cut an hour and 40 minutes out, which necessitated the reinvention of many of the transitions between the two time-frames of the story. The internal chronology of each of the two stories—the present in the monastery, and the past in the desert—was not fundamentally different, but how the two of them blended with each other, how that particular deck of cards got shuffled, changed significantly. In the script, there were perhaps 40 transitions, and five of them remained as they were originally, but the other 35 had to be reinvented because so much time had been removed. We were always on the search for new aural and visual transitions, because if you're going to go back and forth that many times, the transitions have to be interesting and entertaining; you can't leave the audience feeling, "Oh my god, here we go again." By way of comparison, in **The Godfather: Part III** there

were originally fourteen time transitions, but after previewing the film, Francis reduced the number to seven.

Because I mix sound as well as edit picture, I sometimes have this image of myself on a football field, playing both quarterback and a wide receiver at the same time. In editing picture and sketching out the sound, I can anticipate what I will probably be able to do six months later, when we mix the film. (The only other person I know who also does both these jobs is Ben Burtt, and the curious thing is that we have the same birthday, July 12. Make of that what you will!) But the whole nature of filmmaking, after all, is collaborative. I wouldn't want to push this one-man-band idea too far—I love working with other people and sometimes achieving that miraculous collision of ideas which makes the finished film something greater than the sum of its parts.

Anne Voase Coates

"Generally speaking, I just cut the way I feel.
I like to think I'm an actor's editor; I go very
much by the performances."

Anne Voase Coates initially wanted to be a film director, an aspiration frowned upon by her uncle, the famed British film entrepreneur J. Arthur Rank, who assumed she was only in it for the glamour and the good-looking actors. But Coates was persistent enough in her passion that Rank eventually found her a job at a production company specializing in religious films. There, Coates learned to project footage, record sound, and splice scenes, and she eventually became an assistant film editor at London's Pinewood Studios.

Coates received her first editing credit on Noel Langley's **The Pickwick Papers** (1952), ten years before cutting the film that won her an Academy Award, David Lean's epic **Lawrence of Arabia** (1962). She went on to receive four more Oscar nominations for her work on Peter Glenville's **Becket** (1964), David Lynch's **The Elephant Man** (1980), Wolfgang Petersen's **In the Line of Fire** (1993), and Steven Soderbergh's **Out of Sight** (1998). Her other editing credits include **Young Cassidy** (1965), **The Bofors Gun** (1968), **The Public Eye** (1972), **Murder on the Orient Express** (1974), **The Legend of Tarzan, Lord of the Apes** (1984), **What About Bob?** (1991), **Chaplin** (1992), **Congo** (1995), **Striptease** (1996), **Erin Brockovich** (2000), and **Unfaithful** (2002). Coates remains active in Hollywood, having recently co-edited **The Golden Compass** (2007) and edited **Extraordinary Measures** (2010).

Anne Voase Coates

" People often ask me if I have a style of editing. I usually say I don't, but one day my daughter said, "Oh yes, you do. We were studying it in class." So perhaps I do. Everyone has a certain style, but I do try to adapt mine to whatever picture I'm working on. I don't want people to see my films and say, oh yes, that was cut by Anne Coates.

I remember cutting a few test sequences on **Lawrence of Arabia** (1962), and David Lean asked me during dailies, with the whole crew present, if I had finished cutting the first scene. I said I had, and he asked me to bring it down and show him. I said I couldn't possibly show it to him in front of all these people, but he said, "Don't be so silly, just go and get it." I was terrified. I sat there watching, and I don't think I saw a cut go by; I was so frightened. When it was over, David got up and said, "I think that's the first time in my life that I've seen a piece of film cut exactly the way I would have done it," which was the best compliment I had ever had in my life. I was stunned, absolutely stunned.

In the script, we had always intended to dissolve from the shot of Lawrence blowing out the match to the first shot of the desert. We marked a dissolve, but when we watched the footage in the theater, we saw it as a direct cut. David and I both thought, "Wow, that's really interesting." So we decided to nibble at it, taking a few frames off here and there. David looked at it and said, "It's nearly perfect. Take it away, Annie, just make it perfect." So I took literally two frames off, and he said, "That's it."

If I had been working digitally, I would never have seen those two shots cut together like that. We would have done the optical in the machine, and when we took it into the screening room the dissolve already would have been there, so we never would have seen it as a direct cut. I like to think we would have gotten the idea anyway. But another director would not necessarily have seen it or liked it. Luckily, David and I thought alike.

Sometimes it works the other way. **Congo** (1995) was the first film I ever edited digitally. I had been planning to use direct cuts in some of the jungle footage, but I was playing around with the new system and thought I would try some dissolves. They looked so good, and the shots crossed in a really elegant way, so I kept them in. But if I had edited that on film, I probably would have ended up using direct cuts; I would not have sent it away to the lab to have a dissolve done. It was the same thing with **Out to Sea** (1997)— when I cut the dancing montage, I used diagonal dissolves, and they worked really well. I tried all sorts of things that were fun to do, things you could never have done on film.

I loved cutting on film. To me, it was always more personal than it ever is or ever will be on

LAWRENCE OF ARABIA
Coates and **Lawrence of Arabia** director David Lean originally intended to dissolve from a shot of Peter O'Toole blowing out a match to a shot of the sun rising over the desert. But when they viewed the footage, with the dissolve marked but not completed, the transition appeared as a direct cut. They liked the effect so much that they decided to keep it. "It was so dramatically right," Coates says. "You just felt that when you saw it."

digital. I made my first cut on a Moviola with just my little screen and me, with nobody else looking over my shoulder. I felt much more closely involved with it, in a way that I never experience on digital. Back in those days, I never spliced my own film. People used to scoff at me, in a nice way, because most editors spliced their film and then had a look at it. But I would get my assistant to splice it, and then I'd run the scene in the screening room with my crew, and I'd tell them, "Now, don't worry about the cuts. I can smooth the bumps out. I want to know if you find it amusing, if you follow the storytelling, if you like the performances…I just want you to look at it like a real audience." Sometimes they came up with some really good ideas, but they weren't necessarily my ideas. I just found that seeing it on a big screen like that left me with really good impressions.

I suppose I cut differently now, on the Avid, but I get much the same result as I did on film. There may be a few more cuts, but I like to think the story I'm telling and the emotion I'm trying to get out of the scene would be the same either way. I did have some trouble adapting to working digitally. But I said to myself, "Well, it's only a tool. You're telling the same story and going for the same laughs and the same action." Once I could get that into my mind properly and just tell the story, I sailed ahead. I was stumbling for a time, but I was determined to do it. I had thought I

would never actually have to adapt to it in my lifetime, but when the older editors started converting, Jim Clark and other great friends of mine, I realized that I would have to learn, too.

I was so spoiled on **Lawrence of Arabia**. Fantastic stuff was coming in every day. There would be thousands of feet of film, of battle scenes from four cameras, or shots of the huge open desert with camels or a mirage or something. I suppose if I had thought about it too much, I would have been daunted, but I just went right into it. I just cut the story, to be honest. I suppose if I had a choice between a shot with an actor against a great background and a closer shot of the actor, I would have used the former. But basically, I just went with the performances as I always do; the background is always there. I suppose the film could have been a little tighter, but we tried tightening it up when we did the 1989 reconstruction and we didn't like what we did, so we put it back.

Becket (1964) was an interesting film to cut after **Lawrence of Arabia**. Peter Glenville shot **Becket** completely differently, rather stagily in a way, and there wasn't nearly as much footage. It was such a different experience, and to begin with I thought, "God, this stuff's awful. It's got no expanse, no nothing." Until I realized what a good script it was, and how wonderful the dialogue was, and then of course, once I got into it, I →

changed my mind. Peter was a very good director, and he knew what he wanted, and I realized that he was limiting his number of shots because he didn't want Hal Wallis, the producer, to play around with it too much afterward.

Hal wanted to see each sequence cut about two days after Peter Glenville had shot it. And I said, "Well, Peter won't have any time to choose his cut and make his choice of dailies," and Hal said, "He won't be making the choice. I will." And I thought, no way. I felt strongly that at this stage, it should be the director's cut. I managed to contrive it so that I would wait until Peter had made his choice of takes, and I always cut with his choices, not Hal's, and Hal never noticed. It was funny, because he was so adamant about using his takes, and yet he never noticed that I always used Peter's. Because I had only one day to do it in, that helped me learn to cut very quickly. I was always up to date with my cutting, and I was known to be very fast.

When I started reading the script of **The Elephant Man** (1980), I thought, there's no way I'm going to be able to cut this, looking at that face on my Moviola every day. But then I read on, and by the time I reached the end I was in tears, and I thought, there's no way I can't cut this film. He's very brilliant, David Lynch. But we did have a few problems, one being the decision of when to reveal the Elephant Man's head without his hood for the first time. There were two ways to do this: early in the movie, when Treves first visits the Elephant Man at the sideshow, or later, when the Elephant Man is in the hospital and the young nurse drops her tray when she sees him. Mel Brooks, the producer, asked David to shoot both ways. But David, being David, decided to shoot only the way he liked, which was the sideshow scene. Mel was furious, because he had wanted it the other way; he and everyone else thought it would be more dramatic to not see the head until the nurse does.

THE ELEPHANT MAN

One of the key decisions on **The Elephant Man** was when to show the audience the face of the title character (played by John Hurt). David Lynch wanted the audience to see the head the first time Treves (Anthony Hopkins) does, at the sideshow, but producer Mel Brooks insisted that it not be revealed until later. Hurt was mostly kept in shadow during the sideshow sequence, and Coates cut to a single tear rolling down Treves' cheek to suggest the character's deformed appearance. Though an elegant solution, this caused Coates considerable trouble in subsequent scenes, forcing her to cut around the Elephant Man's head until the big unveiling.

"I like to have a few little arguments with the director."

Mel eventually won out, and so in the finished film, you don't see the Elephant Man's head in the sideshow scene—you only see him in shadow, and then we cut to a closeup of Treves with just a tear rolling down his cheek. But this posed a major problem, because we had already shot two or three scenes in between in which you saw the head, and so I had to recut those scenes so you didn't see it—by losing a shot or two, or blowing up the shots until he was out of frame, or by making it so dark and grainy that you couldn't see his face. Blowing it up and making it grainy didn't matter in that film, since it was black and white and grainy anyway. We got around the problem. It wasn't neat, but it could have been a complete disaster; they might have had to go back and reshoot.

David had a really good sound man, Alan Splet, who worked on really old equipment. They made some extraordinary sounds, but they also made some weird ones I didn't like. Once we were watching a scene of the circus in the rain, and suddenly there was this "bang!" noise. And just to be irritating, I jumped and said, "God, what's a gun doing in the middle of that sequence?" David said, "Don't you dare complain about Alan's effects, because they're brilliant!" I said, "Well, if it's meant to be a raindrop, but it sounds like a gunshot, why should I not complain, David?" We had a few little situations like that. He was such a nice man, Alan Splet, but he annoyed me inasmuch as he and David were so close that I felt a bit shut out—as they probably meant me to feel.

I like to have a few little arguments with the director. I don't want to be in a situation in which we're never agreeing on anything, but on the other hand, it's nice to have one or two areas where we're not on exactly the same wavelength. I think Carl Reiner once told the story of how an editor lay on his KEM so the director couldn't make an alteration he wanted. I've never gone →

"There are a few editors who really don't give in, and they don't work."

as far as that, but I can be a little obstinate. There's a story the producers of **Out of Sight** (1998) like to tell, about a scene Steven Soderbergh took out at the recommendation of the studio. I was shocked that he took it out, and I fought and fought to get it back in. The producers were quite impressed, because they realized how strongly I felt. Eventually Steven put it back in. Still, most of the time you have to give in because in the end, it's a director's picture. There are a few editors who really don't give in, and they don't work.

I'm a great experimenter; I'm always trying this and trying that. I love working with Adrian Lyne because he's great at trying everything as well.

Even if it works, he's always messing with it; even with scenes he loves, he still has to try them other ways, just in case he finds something better. That's his temperament. At one point, when I was editing **Unfaithful** (2002), I said to Adrian, "That love scene isn't really working." He told me to take it away and see what I could do. Initially, we had always had the first love scene between Diane Lane and Olivier Martinez, followed by the scene of Diane traveling home on the train. There were only a few bits of the love scene that really worked, and I had about five takes of her on the train. So I put them together and intercut them, so that we flash back to the love scene as she's thinking about what she's done. The result was very much

UNFAITHFUL

The shooting script for **Unfaithful** had Connie (Diane Lane) and Paul (Olivier Martinez) make love for the first time, followed by Connie's train ride home. When Coates found herself struggling with the footage in the love scene, director Adrian Lyne gave her permission to experiment. Coates' creative solution was to intercut the love scene and the train ride so that the audience witnesses the sex act through Connie's memories, synthesizing two straightforward sequences into an electric montage of lust, desire, guilt and shame.

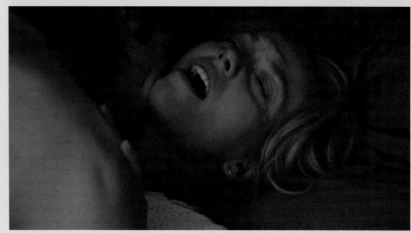

as the final sequence is now. If you can make those things work, great. But I've tried similar things on other films, and they just didn't work.

I think you have to be very careful not to overdo sequences of that sort. On **Out of Sight**, for instance, we had so many flashbacks, so many clever scenes, that one day I said to Steven, "I think we've overdone this." I've said this to other directors: You've gone too far. You've got to stop. Often if something's not working, people will put more cuts or shots in, and it's almost always better to take shots out and calm it down. If something doesn't seem quite right and you don't really know why, simplify. That's something I've learned through trial and error. →

Starting out as Editor...

David Lean: Long before he made **Lawrence of Arabia** and **The Bridge on the River Kwai**, director David Lean was considered one of the top editors in the field. By 1942, when he moved into directing, he had edited more than 20 pictures, including **As You Like It** (1936), **Pygmalion** (1938), **Major Barbara** (1941), **49th Parallel** (1941) and **One of Our Aircraft is Missing** (1942). Lean always maintained that cutting was his first love in filmmaking, and capped his career by editing as well as writing and directing 1984's **A Passage to India**, for which he received Academy Award nominations in all three categories.

Robert Wise: He had edited a dozen pictures before he moved into directing in 1944, including **The Hunchback of Notre Dame** (1939), **The Devil and Daniel Webster** (1941) and Orson Welles' **Citizen Kane** (1941), which earned him an Oscar nomination for editing. He is less fondly remembered for his work on Welles' **The Magnificent Ambersons** (1944), from which, at the insistence of RKO executives, Wise removed 50 minutes of footage which were subsequently destroyed, sealing **The Magnificent Ambersons'** reputation forever as a tarnished masterpiece.

Anthony Harvey: He edited two Stanley Kubrick pictures, **Lolita** (1962) and **Dr. Strangelove or: How I Learned to Stop Worrying and Love the Bomb** (1964), as well as **I'm All Right Jack** (1959), and **The Spy Who Came in From the Cold** (1965).

Hal Ashby: He received more Academy recognition as an editor than as a director, winning for his work on Norman Jewison's **In the Heat of the Night** (1967) and receiving a nomination for **The Russians Are Coming! The Russians Are Coming!** (1966). His other cutter credits include **The Loved One** (1965), **The Cincinnati Kid** (1965) and **The Thomas Crown Affair** (1968).

Nowadays, the directors don't always give you a master shot that you can play long. If the acting is great, why cut in? If it's not broken, don't mend it. I like being able to hold a shot. It doesn't have to be static; it can be a moving shot, so long as it shows the people in the space and captures the performances. Nowadays, that's not fashionable. The more inexperienced directors tend to cut, cut, cut—they go right in immediately.

It's so personal, cutting. I find it very difficult to discuss. Walter Murch can explain why he cuts where he cuts, but I can't. Generally speaking, I just cut the way I feel. I like to think I'm an actor's editor; I go very much by the performances. I'm also known as an emotional cutter. One of the best compliments I ever had was from Carol Reed, when I was editing his last film, **The Public Eye** (1972). "There's a lot of really good editors," he said. "But you're the one with the most heart." I thought that was lovely. I've always treasured that. "

OUT OF SIGHT
At a certain point while cutting together the flashbacks in **Out of Sight**, Coates told director Steven Soderbergh that she thought the film was becoming rather top-heavy with flashbacks and structural gimmicks. "I said to Steven, 'I think we've overdone this.' There were too many clever scenes," she says. "I've said this to other directors: You've gone too far. You've got to stop. If something doesn't seem quite right and you don't really know why, simplify."

IN THE LINE OF FIRE

The telephone call between Secret Service agent Frank Horrigan (Clint Eastwood) and assassin Mitch Leary (John Malkovich) in Wolfgang Petersen's **In the Line of Fire** posed a considerable challenge in the cutting room. "You wanted to see them both, but we didn't want to go into that sort of split-screen business," says Coates. To maintain emotional continuity through the sequence, she tried to ensure that a cut to one actor would complete or continue an expression from his previous shot. Further complicating the sequence, Malkovich had to remain only partly visible and images from the Kennedy assassination had to be superimposed over Eastwood's haunted visage.

Richard Marks

"You need to set the tone early on. If you give the audience a path, chances are they're going to follow it."

A native New Yorker born in 1943, Richard Marks was fortunate enough to begin his prolific editing career as a protégé of Dede Allen, whom he assisted on such Arthur Penn films as **Alice's Restaurant** (1969) and **Little Big Man** (1970), and with whom he co-edited Sidney Lumet's **Serpico** (1973). After cutting Francis Ford Coppola's **The Godfather: Part II** (1974) with Barry Malkin and Peter Zinner, Marks received his first Academy Award nomination for his work as a member of the editing team on Coppola's **Apocalypse Now** (1979).

Marks has edited all six features written and directed by James L. Brooks, and received three additional Oscar nominations for his work on Brooks' **Terms of Endearment** (1983), **Broadcast News** (1987) and **As Good as It Gets** (1997). His other editor credits include Elia Kazan's **The Last Tycoon** (1976), Herbert Ross' **Pennies From Heaven** (1981), Cameron Crowe's **Say Anything...** (1989), Warren Beatty's **Dick Tracy** (1990) and the Nora Ephron comedies **You've Got Mail** (1998) and **Julie & Julia** (2009).

Richard Marks

"I had no idea how I was going to earn a living when I graduated. I was working various jobs and trying to avoid grad school, and I was terribly bored until a friend of mine suggested I get into the film business. A family friend who worked at United Artists was able to get me a job at a release printhouse in New York, and with that job came the promise of an editor gig. I had no idea if I was even interested in editing, but it seemed like a path, and desperate people grasp onto paths.

Something seemed to click from the very beginning, and after a year or two of cutting commercials and trailers, I decided to try and make a move into features. I soon found that working in dramatic films required me to draw on everything that had interested me as an English lit major, which is story and character. If editing is anything, it's telling a story and applying a rhythm to that story. Whether it's writing a story or editing a film, the process that happens is very similar.

I was Dede Allen's assistant on **Alice's Restaurant** (1969), and when that was finished she asked me to continue with her on Arthur Penn's next film, **Little Big Man** (1970). At that time, the film business in New York was much more fluid than the Hollywood studio system. As an assistant, you could become an editor in a reasonably quick period of time. And I started out right at a time when a lot of movies were being made, and a lot of young directors were storming Old Hollywood, so there were many opportunities for advancement. I was lucky. I presume I had some talent, but I was lucky.

Dede was amazing. She was born to teach, and for me, it was an incredible learning process. I know what it's like to teach, and Dede had a much greater level of tolerance than I will probably ever have. She was a very patient woman. And editing was a very different process back then, a much more physical, labor-intensive process. There were always competing ways of organizing material: There was the Moviola school

I'LL DO ANYTHING

Marks had planned to use two editing systems to cut Brooks' **I'll Do Anything**: traditional film for the dramatic portions, and the George Lucas EditDroid for the more complex multi-camera musical sequences. When Brooks decided to scrap the musical numbers altogether and do significant reshoots, Marks found himself testing out a third platform, the Avid, to edit the reshot material. "From the moment I used it, I was hooked. It was an incredible tool," Marks says, though he also notes, "I always wanted Jim to let us redo **I'll Do Anything** as a musical, as it was originally intended."

> **"…there were many problems, system crashes and lost cuts, and every night the assistant had to stay to back up the system on floppy disks."**

and the flatbed editing school. Dede hailed from the Moviola school, and ultimately, digital editing became an almost exact extrapolation of that method. On the Avid, you're putting things into bins and breaking them down into individual takes, much as we did with film.

The first time I used the Avid was on James L. Brooks' **I'll Do Anything** (1994). Because the film was originally going to be a musical, requiring multiple cameras and multiple playback, I decided to use two methods: I would cut the dramatic portions on film, and I would cut the musical sequences on the George Lucas EditDroid, a laserdisc-based system that was subject to massive mechanical failures and had maybe a two-minute linear memory. But the attraction of the system was that for the musical numbers, you could look at four cameras simultaneously and make edits from one camera to another, which I thought would save me a lot of time. Ultimately it did, but toward the end of that film, we decided it wasn't going to be a musical anymore, and planned about seven or eight days of reshoots.

At the time, Avid was really trying to promote its equipment, specifically the fact that it could handle a lot more material than before. (The system had been used extensively in commercials and music videos, but it had been incapable of coordinating enough memory to make it feasible for feature editing.) It was also incredibly expensive. I told them, if you want me to try it, I'll try it, but you've got to give it to me for free; we can't afford it. So they set up an Avid system in my cutting room, which meant that now I was working in three formats. I cut all the reshoots on the Avid, and I have to say, from the moment I used it, I was hooked. It was an incredible tool, and you could already see the writing on the wall; it was only a matter of time before it took over. I decided from then on, if I was going to cut a film, it had to be part of the agreement that they allow me to cut it on the Avid.

Which is not to say that it wasn't frustrating at first. It was difficult and clumsy. I was computer-ignorant, so I wasn't just adjusting to a new cutting system; I was adapting to this whole world of computers. Plus, the Avid was obviously not as sophisticated as it is now; there were many problems, system crashes and lost cuts, and every night the assistant had to stay to back up the system on floppy disks.

But with editing, you have to be open to change. I mean, that's what the process is all about. If you aren't willing to change, you shouldn't be editing. I know editors who found the new technology difficult. There was a lot of grumbling initially, a lot of resistance. Their attitude was, "Well, I've done it this way, so this must be the right way to do it," which is insane. You shouldn't be doing it if that's your attitude.

People often ask what style I use. I think the best answer is that the material should dictate the style. You can violate that as much as you want; you can slow down a fast cut and lose the drama, or you can kill a comedy by cutting it too slowly. But it's the material itself that has to guide you into the style.

For instance, on **The Godfather: Part II** (1974), Francis Ford Coppola had always intended to use lengthy dissolves between scenes. Where those dissolves would occur changed constantly, but the stylistic decision to use dissolves was made fairly early on; it was so very fitting for that kind of interplay of multiple stories. I spent months on those dissolves. We used what was called an A-and-B negative, which preserved the integrity of the look of the original negative. We experimented endlessly with lengths of dissolves, and we played around with where they went in the story. That was the whole finishing process on that film, deciding where we went, when we went there, and how much of one story we could tell without losing the audience.

I was one of three editors on **The Godfather: Part II**, and when you're trading off like that, your styles begin to homogenize, as they should. As much as you might want to control something, you have to just give it up. **Apocalypse Now** (1979) was that way, too. I was the supervising editor, and I was just one of four credited editors, though there were others who worked on the →

THE GODFATHER: PART II

Dissolving from one scene to the next—a technique that can be achieved now with the click of a mouse—proved much more laborious and time-consuming in the days of cutting on film. At the time when Richard Marks was editing **The Godfather: Part II**, the process could be accomplished using one of two methods: single-strand opticals, which required an optical house to produce a new negative for the section in question, and A/B opticals, which used the original negative and thus saved a generation of grain.

The dissolves in Francis Ford Coppola's picture were especially complex in part due to their lengthy duration, signifying not merely a transition between scenes but a transition in time, and establishing thematic parallels between past and present. Early on, the film fades from a shot of young Vito Corleone, having just arrived in turn-of-the-century New York from Sicily, to a shot of his grandson Anthony several decades later. Later in the picture, an image of Michael at Anthony's bedside transitions into a flashback to Vito's early family life.

editing as well. So many of us worked on that film and fell by the wayside over the course of it. But it emerged with a very specific style, and part of that was our ability to juggle and trade off scenes. Even when you're editing individual pieces of a film, it's important to serve the entire overall structure. Otherwise, the pieces are meaningless and you're floundering. In many ways, on **Apocalypse Now**, there was a lot of floundering. At one point, all the on-set dramatic scenes and action scenes had been shot, but none of the connective material—the narration, the scenes of Martin Sheen going up the river, none of that had been shot. We had no connective tissue, and we had to build it over the course of three years. It was an insane process, a mind-boggling experience. The footage was endless. I like to say that everybody went on that journey upriver to find Kurtz, including all of us. We went into the heart of darkness.

As an editor, I'm very performance-driven. I love the shadings you can get when you manipulate the tone of a character, just by what you use in the cut. But you can't make a bad performance a great one. The editing process is almost limitless in the number of manipulations you can perform, but it isn't magic.

When I was first working with Jim Brooks, on **Terms of Endearment** (1983), there was one original cast member, in a minor role, who struck me as not quite right. When I saw the first dailies, I was…disturbed. I didn't really know what to do. I have a big mouth and I tend to say what I think, but I didn't know Jim well, as we had only been working together for a couple of months. In the end I decided it would be dishonest of me not to say something, so I called him and said, "I don't know how to say this, and I may be totally wrong, but this is my impression of this actor." And Jim listened very carefully, and that weekend he recast the part.

All this did, of course, was reinforce my big mouth. But I assume that's what I'm hired for. Some directors I've worked with really don't want to know my opinions. Others do. I think →

Vito & Michael & Julie & Julia

Few films might seem more dissimilar at first than Francis Ford Coppola's epic gangster drama **The Godfather: Part II** and Nora Ephron's frothy culinary comedy **Julie & Julia**. But the fact that both pictures were edited by Marks—and both required him to juxtapose two storylines set in different time periods—demands a closer study.

The Godfather: Part II remains, in Marks' estimation, "the best example of juggling stories in a film. The modern story had a very up pace, and the old story in Sicily and early New York had a much more legato feel. We always hit that wall of having to balance the thrust and the energy of those two stories. And that became one of the more complicated things we had to accomplish, keeping the balance and keeping the story moving, and not letting the audience hit a wall or get tired of the rhythmic changes.

"It was a very dangerous structure at the time. It was not in fashion, and it was burdened with the fact that it was a sequel. The interesting thing about **The Godfather: Part II** is that it was a much more serious, intellectual film than its predecessor. That's fascinating, in that it was the very opposite of what sequels have become."

Julie & Julia "was a difficult challenge in that Julie was not a very sympathetic character in any way. There's a certain irritation value to Julie—in contrast to Julia Child, who's so endearing. There were many passages where we had to back away from Julie, so that the audience would maintain some sort of sympathy with her. There's something very frenetic and neurotic about the Julie story, and the period-piece section with Julia is so much more legato. It's always interesting to try and balance that. You never know how it's going to go together until you start to screen it and see how long it holds."

TERMS OF ENDEARMENT

Marks and James L. Brooks initially tried test-screening a version of **Terms of Endearment** without its opening scene, in which Aurora (Shirley MacLaine) awakens her infant daughter to make sure she hasn't been a victim of "crib death." They found the film wasn't nearly as effective without that amusing and faintly appalling prologue. "Without that key, it took too long for the audience to get into the story, and they didn't understand Shirley's character; they just found her strangely abusive," Marks says.

> **"You can't make a bad performance a great one. The editing process is almost limitless in the number of manipulations you can perform, but it isn't magic."**

my success in working with Jim is that there's an honesty in how we deal with each other. Jim is great in that he can absorb other people's opinions and not feel under attack. Many people feel under attack when they hear an opinion that's contrary to theirs. The director–editor relationship really is like dating. Jim and I are well into the marriage, more than 30 years later.

One of the experiments we tried on **Terms of Endearment** was to screen a version without the opening shot, which changed people's perceptions of the movie enormously. That first shot of Shirley MacLaine's character pinching her baby in the crib to wake her up—it just told you how to take the rest of the movie. Without that key, it took too long for the audience to get into the story, and they didn't understand Shirley's character; they just found her strangely abusive. Personally, the experiment taught me how important those first few moments are, and what it means to set up audience expectations at the beginning of a film. You need to set the tone →

BROADCAST NEWS

For **Broadcast News**, Marks amassed an enormous library of stock news footage to be played on the numerous screens in the TV studio. Because shots and angles were changing constantly, the material had to be available to drop in at a moment's notice; for this reason, the special-report sequence, in which Tom (William Hurt) takes over the anchor's chair for the first time, proved especially complex from a technical and logistical point of view. "It was enormously fun, but a lot of complicated work," Marks says. "There was a lot of footage, much more than on **Terms of Endearment**. I think the amount of footage gets incrementally larger as the process becomes cheaper."

early on. If you give the audience a path, chances are they're going to follow it.

I came onto **Broadcast News** (1987) very early and started researching all the stock footage that we used on screens in the background. I developed this enormous library of material and set it up so it could be used at a moment's notice, because shots and angles always change. Technically, it was very demanding. Cutting what we called the "special report" sequence, when William Hurt's character gets to be anchor for the first time, was enormously fun, but immensely complicated work. There was a lot of footage, much more than there had been on **Terms of Endearment.** I think the amount of footage gets larger as the process gets cheaper.

It's interesting how that process has changed. Certainly, digital editing allows you greater and faster access to the material. Sometimes I think the process has become so fast that it doesn't allow you thinking time. The truth is, it hasn't significantly changed the speed with which films are finished. You just wind up doing more versions, because it takes a shorter amount of time to do so. The important thing is to not let the amount of material paralyze you and keep you from making an initial decision about the way you want to go in a scene. It doesn't mean you can't reverse direction, but at some point, you have to take a point of view and follow it, even if you wind up changing it a million times.

Films are cut and paced more quickly now,

SAY ANYTHING...

One of the key challenges on **Say Anything...** (1989) was to keep a key fact about John Mahoney's character a secret for most of the film, yet also to make the revelation seem organic enough in terms of character development that it wouldn't come as a complete surprise. "There were moments when you had to avoid a sidelong glance or some kind of look or reaction that would nail him as the villain," Marks says. "If you're trying to parcel out what you know about a character, that build becomes very important—when you cut to them, how long you stay with them, etc. It's so important to know where you're going."

> **"At some point, you have to take a point of view and follow it, even if you wind up changing it a million times."**

because that's a reflection of the society we live in, which is much more about instant gratification, and it demands a pace that the audience will feel comfortable with. I mean, just look at a film like **The Social Network**, which is very fast-paced in a way that's appropriate to the material and its audience. The other night, I was watching a film I'd edited, and I thought to myself, I could never pace a film like that again. No one would ever go to see it. I'm serious. Your expectations and your internal sense of rhythm change. And unless you let them change, you become obsolete in terms of being able to present entertainment to a contemporary audience. 🙶

PENNIES FROM HEAVEN
Herbert Ross' Depression-era musical **Pennies From Heaven** was so poorly received in its initial previews that Ross and Marks set about trying to overhaul the picture—primarily by lightening the darkness of Steve Martin's character, which audiences had rejected because it didn't jive with the actor's wild-and-crazy Saturday Night Live persona. MGM had invested a considerable amount of money in the production and was desperate for a hit. "We kept making changes, shooting additional material, drawing up storyboards and going out on previews. Nothing helped," Marks recalls. Finally, Herb had the balls to say, "I don't know what we're doing to this movie. We're massacring it." The film was released in the form Ross had intended it to be released, and while it was far from a box office success, it retains its ardent champions to this day.

Peter Zinner

A Hollywood renaissance man, Peter Zinner was a producer, a music editor and supervisor, an actor (he played Admiral Padorin in 1990's **The Hunt for Red October**) and a director (of the 1981 thriller **The Salamander**). But it is his prolific career as a film and TV editor that has proved to be his most enduring legacy, particularly his work on such seminal 1970s' pictures as Francis Ford Coppola's **The Godfather** (1972) and **The Godfather: Part II** (1974), and the film that won him the Academy Award for best editing, Michael Cimino's **The Deer Hunter** (1978).

Born to Jewish parents in Vienna in 1919, Zinner fled the Nazis with his family in 1938, moving to the Philippines before arriving in Los Angeles two years later, where he sought a job in the film industry. After working as a taxi driver and playing the piano in silent movie theaters, he became an apprentice film editor at 20th Century Fox in 1943 and eventually an assistant sound-effects editor at Universal, eventually parlaying these gigs into work as a music editor at studios including MGM. He received his first music-editing credit, appropriately enough, on **For the First Time** (1959), director Rudolph Maté's drama about an opera singer (played by tenor Mario Lanza).

While Zinner worked as a music editor on several subsequent pictures including Samuel Fuller's **The Naked Kiss** (1964) and Richard Brooks' **Lord Jim** (1965), he eventually shifted his attentions toward picture-editing. The first film he edited, Brooks' 1964 western **The Professionals** (1966), earned him an ACE Eddie Award nomination. Zinner went on to cut Brooks' 1967 adaptation of Truman Capote's **In Cold Blood**, as well as Blake Edwards' **Darling Lili** (1970) and Mikhail Kalatozov's **The Red Tent** (1969).

01 The Godfather: Part II
02 The Godfather
03 The Deer Hunter

Zinner received his first Oscar nomination for **The Godfather**, sharing the honor with his co-editor, William Reynolds. The film's celebrated climactic montage, which intercuts the baptism of Michael Corleone's son with the murders of the other heads of the Five Families, remains one of Zinner's most masterful editorial achievements; his strong musical background served him well here, as it was his decision to have the church organ play over the sequence, lending it much of its dramatic power and moral irony.

He edited **The Godfather: Part II** with Barry Malkin and Richard Marks, and their work on the film, with its complex past-and-present structure, earned them a BAFTA nomination. Zinner went on to cut Berry Gordy's **Mahogany** (1975), Arturo Ripstein's **Foxtrot** (1976), and Frank Pierson's **A Star Is Born** (1976). He faced the unenviable challenge of whittling down Cimino's Vietnam War drama **The Deer Hunter** to a 183-minute theatrical version (the initial cut ran three-and-a-half hours), a task that won him not only the Oscar but a BAFTA and an Eddie Award.

He earned a final Oscar nomination for editing Taylor Hackford's popular romantic weepie **An Officer and a Gentleman** (1982), and the later phase of his career was largely devoted to television, including such miniseries as **The Winds of War** (1983) and **War and Remembrance** (1988), and numerous telefilms including **Citizen Cohn** (1992), **The Enemy Within** (1994), **Dirty Pictures** (2000) and **Conspiracy** (2001). He received four Emmy nominations and two wins, for **War and Remembrance** and **Citizen Cohn**.

Zinner received his final editing credit in collaboration with his daughter, Katina, on **Running With Arnold** (2006), Dan Cox's documentary about Arnold Schwarzenegger's California run. He died at the age of 88 in 2007 from complications of non-Hodgkin's lymphoma.

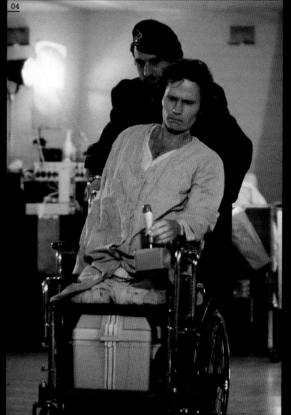

04 The Deer Hunter

05 The Deer Hunter

06 An Officer and a Gentle

Stephen Mirrione

"I sometimes look at performances in other movies and come away thinking, that director really didn't protect that actor. I'm very aware of the sacredness of the trust I'm being given in terms of an actor's performance."

It was during his film classes at University of California, Santa Cruz, that Stephen Mirrione decided he wanted to edit features for a living. In 1991, he moved to Los Angeles and became friends with Doug Liman, who was then working on his graduate thesis film at USC and already had a cutting room set up at Disney. It was soon after that Mirrione edited Liman's first feature, **Getting In** (1994), before going on to cut his **Swingers** (1996) and **Go** (1999).

At the age of 32, Mirrione received the Academy Award for editing Steven Soderbergh's **Traffic** (2000), which marked the beginning of a collaboration that includes **Ocean's Eleven** (2001), **Ocean's Twelve** (2004), **Ocean's Thirteen** (2007), and **The Informant!** (2009). He has also enjoyed key working relationships with several other filmmakers, having edited Alejandro González Iñárritu's **21 Grams** (2003), **Babel** (2006, with Douglas Crise), and **Biutiful** (2010); George Clooney's **Confessions of a Dangerous Mind** (2002), **Good Night, and Good Luck** (2005), and **Leatherheads** (2008); Jill Sprecher's **Clockwatchers** (1997), **Thirteen Conversations About One Thing** (2001) and **The Convincer** (2011). He is currently at work on Soderbergh's action-thriller **Contagion** (2011) and George Clooney's political drama **Ides of March** (2011).

Stephen Mirrione

" There is an alchemy in film editing that is difficult to articulate, partly because so few people are even aware of it. It's a common misconception that editing a film is like editing an essay or a newspaper, that its primary purpose is to determine content. In fact, it's completely its own discipline. Obviously it's heavily influenced by music, rhythm, movement within the frame, and emotion. As an editor, you are largely molding and shaping the emotional content of a scene and affecting the point of view of the audience.

I had always been interested in storytelling and writing, particularly the way, psychologically, you could manipulate language to send the reader in one direction or another. I had also played the viola growing up, so I knew from an early age that it's never enough just to like something or be good at it; if you want to master something, you have to practice. When I was taking film classes in college, I soon realized editing was the one part of the process that I had the discipline to do over and over again. So I really threw myself into it and practiced, practiced, practiced.

I learned a lot when I was editing Doug Liman's first film, **Getting In** (1994)—such as how to change written dialogue in a way that it doesn't feel as though it was changed, and how to motivate a cut if I didn't get quite the angles I wanted. I really appreciated the fact that we were cutting on film. They were shooting on 35mm stock, and I was using a KEM, which forced a certain discipline. The physicality of it made you really think about what you were doing before you did it.

An important moment came when I was cutting **Swingers** (1996), specifically the sequence when Vince Vaughn and Jon Favreau arrive in Las Vegas. I found this big-band music I liked that was really big and bold. They had shot all these animated neon signs, and in one particular shot of the Westward Ho marquee, I got the lion's tail to snap in exact sync with the music. Something just clicked for me in that moment. What I realized was that these two guys are getting to Vegas, and they're feeling that excitement and energy of life the same way I am right here, in this moment, in this little room. I ended up staying in the cutting room all night, driven by that high, and I knew that when I was done, it was going to be a finished thing, not a first draft, and it was going to be amazing.

The next afternoon, I showed Doug the scene,

SWINGERS

The Las Vegas arrival sequence in **Swingers** proved a crucial one for then-fledgling editor Stephen Mirrione, who conveyed the energy of the Strip by cutting rapidly from one glittering casino to the next, all set to brassy big-band rhythms. Mirrione found himself experiencing the same rush that Trent (Vince Vaughn) and Mike (Jon Favreau) must have been feeling. "When I go back to it, I'm not really watching the scene," Mirrione recalls. "I'm remembering the night I put it together and achieved that personal milestone of knowing that, yes, I am an editor."

"It's a common misconception that editing a film is like editing an essay or a newspaper."

and of course his reaction was, "Eh?" He wasn't wrong; it was a natural first reaction. When you're editing, you're taking an emotional journey, and when you show it to someone who's got a very clear idea of what it's going to be, they haven't taken that emotional journey with you. You've got to be sensitive to that as an editor. Luckily, within 10 minutes, Vince and Jon came barreling in, and when I showed it to them, they just leapt out of their seats. They were flipping out. The finished sequence in the film is, frame for frame, exactly what happened that night. When I go back to it, I'm not really watching the scene; I'm remembering the night I put it together and achieved that personal milestone of knowing that, yes, I am an editor.

It was a big leap to go from with working with Doug to working with Steven Soderbergh on **Traffic** (2000). Doug and I had been learning together as we went along, but suddenly I was working with someone who was such a master at understanding what a scene is about, who knew how to shoot a scene for editing, specifically how to create coverage for these moments. Because there was so much material and so many great choices in terms of how to put it together, the big challenge for me was to find a way to limit my choices.

With **Traffic**, the trick I used to keep myself from going crazy was to imagine the film as a documentary, with only one camera in any given scene, and therefore any cut I made had to be possible within those confines, as if the cameraman had been able to turn and get another angle. It would've been very easy for me to cut from the looser B camera to the tighter A camera without any discontinuity, but having this other condition in place forced me to consider other takes, and it helped me find moments I might otherwise not have found.

A lot of people ask me about the party/overdose sequence in **Traffic**, because it's very flashy editorially. After Steven and I had worked on it for a while, he asked me if I could start using quicker and quicker cuts. I decided it would be exciting to go in there like a jazz musician, as →

TRAFFIC

For the party/overdose sequence in **Traffic**, Mirrione and Steven Soderbergh opted to quicken the film's pulse, something they achieved by deploying rapid-fire dissolves from one shot to the next. Mirrione says, "I wanted it to feel more out of control and visceral and build a rhythm that accelerated, but not in a predictable way."

21 GRAMS

Alejandro González Iñárritu spent considerable time shooting a particular scene in **21 Grams**, in which Paul (Sean Penn) drives Cristina (Naomi Watts) home and pulls into her garage. The shoot called for multiple setups and went far past schedule, to the point where some members of the crew questioned Iñárritu's methods. But when Mirrione saw the dailies, he was stunned by the number of emotional beats that the director had managed to capture. "He told such an incredibly complex story through the look on Sean's face, having him look around and see the baby seat and having different angles of Cristina laying there," says Mirrione, who managed to weave these wordless shots into a brief but effective and eloquent sequence. "He was painting with a palette so sophisticated, they just didn't realize what was going on at the time."

opposed to a classical one. So, using the music I had, I started tapping out these offbeat rhythms. I took all the different camera angles and stacked them in the Avid timeline, and I just started snipping out pieces to those rhythms. I had done something similar in the title sequence of **Go** (1999, Liman), and here I wanted to capture the emotion of this overdose moment; I wanted it to feel more out of control and visceral and build a rhythm that accelerated, but not in a predictable way.

After **Traffic** and **Ocean's Eleven** (2001), Steven told me that George Clooney wanted me to edit his first feature, **Confessions of a Dangerous Mind** (2002). George is really, really smart, and it was nice working with an actor-director, because so much of what I'm doing is focused on performance. One of the great things about the directors I've worked with is that they allow their actors to go way out there, take big risks and not be sorry for it later. I sometimes look at performances in other movies and come

away thinking, that director really didn't protect that actor. I'm very aware of the sacredness of the trust I'm being given in terms of an actor's performance.

Even among all the great performances I've worked with, David Strathairn in **Good Night, and Good Luck** (2005, Clooney) stands out. You couldn't take your eyes off him. He was perfect, just perfect. As an editor, if you've got that to work with as your base, every editorial decision you make is going to be golden. A lot of times when you're making a decision to cut, you're trying to join two takes together or hide a flub. But with a performance like Strathairn's, you can throw out all those considerations and cut purely when you and the director want to. For that final Edward R. Murrow broadcast, it was great to be able to sustain that take and just sit with him as the camera's slowly pushing in.

My first film with Alejandro González Iñárritu, **21 Grams** (2003), was difficult, but not because

of the nonlinear structure. What gave me a hard time was finding a cutting style within scenes. Alejandro would immediately call me out if I was using some of the techniques or tricks I had used in **Traffic**, in terms of trying to smooth over cuts and performances. He told me, "You keep editing like a really good editor. I don't want you to do that. I want you to break it." I realized he was asking me to jumble each scene, to splice together the individual moments in the same raw, collage-like way the entire movie is structured. So I shoved pieces together without worrying about having them match or feel continuous. I even put jump cuts in the background music. It was very exciting for me as an artist, having to break down my aesthetic and build it back up again.

In the climactic scene, Benicio Del Toro shows up and bursts into the hotel room where Naomi Watts and Sean Penn are, and there's a struggle. As we were putting the scene together, Alejandro saw that something wasn't working, and I think he was considering reshooting the scene. I suggested that, as the scene was unfolding, we start to stretch it and give it Sean's point of view, and have it become a kind of emotional representation of what he's feeling. Earlier in the movie, we had the sound of a train going by in the distance; I took the sound of that train and laid it over the scene, and very slowly dropped out the ambient sound in the room. It gave us the freedom to have a scene that was completely subjective. That's the kind of magic that can happen in the editing room, but the solution came out of necessity, out of trying to solve a problem. If Alejandro had known he wanted the scene to turn out that way, it would have been shot differently. By coming up with a solution that didn't compromise his vision, we avoided an expensive reshoot.

Because I've worked on a number of movies with multiple storylines and/or nonlinear construction, I get a lot of credit as an editor →

21 GRAMS

After struggling with the climactic scene of **21 Grams**, Iñárritu considered a potentially expensive reshoot until Mirrione suggested that they try to give it a more subjective spin, having the violent events take on Paul's point of view. They achieved this by dropping all dialogue and ambient noise from the scene, replacing them with the sound of a passing train (heard earlier in the film). "That's the kind of magic that can happen in the editing room, but the solution came out of necessity, out of trying to solve a problem," Mirrione says. "If Alejandro had known he wanted the scene to turn out that way, it would have been shot differently."

for elements I really had nothing to do with, such as the arrangement of scenes. That's largely all in the script. The structure of the script is the DNA, the foundation. It's got wiggle room, and you can bend and shift things. But I did just as much structural reworking on, say, a linear story like **Good Night, and Good Luck** as on a multi-narrative epic like **Traffic**.

The first assembly of **Babel** (2006) was pretty much done by the time Alejandro finished shooting, right after Thanksgiving 2005. But in early December, Alejandro came to me and said he wanted to try something. I don't think he trusted the structure anymore; he had become bored with it. So we started completely rearranging it, so that you'd be on a scene, and then you'd shift to Japan, and then you'd shift to Morocco; you'd be shifting around all the time. We did that for about two weeks, and we got

about 20 or 30 minutes in before Alejandro said, "This is ridiculous. This doesn't work at all." So we put it back in its proper structure. The DNA of the movie existed in this original form.

As we were working, the Cannes Film Festival was coming up, and we were wondering if it would be possible for us to make the deadline. I think deep down, Alejandro knew he could work on **Babel** for another year or two. But the danger of that is, let's say you get it to 90 percent perfect. You can spend another year trying to get that last ten percent, and you can maybe get an extra three percent or so, or ruin the movie. It was time to move on. We went crazy trying to get it done in time for Cannes, but we did. I think it was to the movie's advantage that we had a very focused, short window in which to complete it.

My satisfaction comes from an intimate relationship with the movie as it's being born;

from being able to touch the footage, move it around, be alone with it, share that with the director. That dialogue with the director, fine-tuning, sculpting performances, the one-on-one relationship it's simple, but that moment of back and forth is the real, driving satisfaction for me.

As an editor, you're usually committing about a year of your life to a film, and it does become part of your identity. I don't want to have that year go by and feel like I've wasted my time. I tend to choose directors and projects based on character and content, rather than following a financial motivation. I'm not complaining about my compensation, because I do very well in spite of these choices. I'm very aware of how lucky I am that I'm in a position to do meaningful work, and that I've worked with people who find that as important as I do.

The multi-taskers

While Steven Soderbergh is one of Mirrione's regular collaborators, the director has cut a number of his pictures himself, including **Sex, Lies, and Videotape** (1989), **King of the Hill** (1993), **Solaris** (2002), **Bubble** (2005), **The Good German** (2006) and **The Girlfriend Experience** (2009), sometimes billed as Mary Ann Bernard. Soderbergh isn't the only currently working filmmaker to edit his own work.

James Cameron: In addition to writing and directing **Titanic** (1997) and **Avatar** (2009), Cameron served as one of a trio of editors on each film.

Joel and Ethan Coen: Under the pseudonym of Roderick Jaynes, the Coen brothers have edited 12 of their 15 features to date, the exceptions being **Raising Arizona** (1987), **Miller's Crossing** (1990) and **The Hudsucker Proxy** (1994).

Robert Rodriguez: From **El Mariachi** (1992) and **Desperado** (1995) to the three **Spy Kids** movies and **Machete** (2010), Rodriguez has not only edited his own films but also often served as cinematographer, camera operator, composer, production designer, visual effects supervisor and sound editor, earning him the nickname "the one-man film crew."

George A. Romero: The maestro of modern horror edited a number of his early films including **Hungry Wives** (1972), **The Crazies** (1973) and **Dawn of the Dead** (1978). He went uncredited for editing his first feature, the 1968 horror classic **Night of the Living Dead**.

Kevin Smith: The writer-director has edited all his own films (often working with co-editor Scott Mosier) except 1995's **Mallrats**, which was cut by Paul Dixon.

BABEL

Iñárritu tried experimenting with the first assembly of **Babel**, placing the scenes in a different order from the one prescribed by Guillermo Arriaga's intricate script; in the new configuration, the film was far jumpier, shifting constantly from one locale to the next. But after about two weeks of restructuring, he opted to restore the film to its initial order. "There was no other way," Mirrione says. "The DNA of the movie existed in this original form."

For Mirrione, the nightclub scene in **Babel** presented an opportunity for a full sensory immersion in the mind of Tokyo schoolgirl Chieko (Rinko Kikuchi). "The scene was about having this character, who had been so closed off and so distraught and depressed, suddenly experiencing this very intense emotional freedom," Mirrione recalls. To that end, Mirrione resisted the temptation to make the scene merely trippy, instead splicing in point-of-view shots in which the sound dropped out abruptly, simulating the perspective of a deaf person.

Dylan Tichenor

"Nonlinear editing is a huge, tremendous change in our industry and a boon, and it enables us to try many different things and save different versions. But I think some skill and focus can be lost with that freedom. It doesn't encourage deep thinking; it encourages shallow thinking."

Born in 1968 into a family of movie buffs, Philadelphia native Dylan Tichenor decided at an early age that if he wasn't going to be an astronaut, he was going to be a filmmaker. Early on he worked as an assistant in the New York offices of Robert Altman, who introduced him to the editor who would become his longtime mentor, Geraldine Peroni. Dylan assisted Peroni on **The Player** (1992), **Short Cuts** (1993) and **Prêt-à-Porter** (1994) before receiving his first editor credit, with Brent Carpenter, on **Jazz '34** (1997), a companion documentary to Robert Altman's **Kansas City** (1996). He has since edited such features as Anthony Drazan's **Hurlyburly** (1998), M. Night Shyamalan's **Unbreakable** (2000), Wes Anderson's **The Royal Tenenbaums** (2001), Ang Lee's **Brokeback Mountain** (2005), Andrew Dominik's **The Assassination of Jesse James by the Coward Robert Ford** (2007), John Patrick Shanley's **Doubt** (2008), Drew Barrymore's **Whip It** (2009), and Ben Affleck's **The Town** (2010). But his longest and most noteworthy collaboration has been with Paul Thomas Anderson, for whom Tichenor served as post-production supervisor on **Hard Eight** (1996) before going on to edit **Boogie Nights** (1997), **Magnolia** (1999), and **There Will Be Blood** (2007), which earned him an Academy Award nomination and an ACE Eddie Award nomination.

Dylan Tichenor

" When I was ten, my dad showed me Murnau's **Nosferatu**. There's this cut in the film that's emblazoned on my brain. Max Schreck is coming down the hall, and the film cuts away to our hero. Then it cuts back, and Schreck is so much closer than you would expect him to be, opening the door. It freaked me out. Why, though? I knew he was coming to the door, so why did it freak me out? It's because of that little chunk of time that's missing. If they had cut back to him where they had left off, it would have been so normal as to be pedestrian. But by jumping him to the door, the moment took on this whole supernatural air, just by dropping 16 frames or so. It amazed me and got me thinking, at a very early age, about the possibilities of film editing.

My dad had prints of films—Welles movies, Corman movies, 16mm prints and 8mm prints—which I used to pull apart and look at. There was a reel-reduction print of one film, which I always

remember being **The Magnificent Ambersons**, and I would look along the strip of film and see the point where the shot changed from a wide shot to a closeup, which fascinated me. I remember taking scissors, cutting some of the reels apart and hanging them up on pins—I was young and stupid, and didn't know how to edit, but I was really getting into it.

I was working as a P.A. and second assistant director on low-budget features in New York when Bob Altman's producer, Scotty Bushnell, asked if I wanted to come out to L.A. to be apprentice editor on **The Player**. Gerri Peroni, Bob's editor, wasn't sure she wanted to give me the job—I think she thought I was too green. But she eventually agreed, and I spent about five years working with her and Bob, during which I also worked as associate editor on Alan Rudolph's **Mrs. Parker and the Vicious Circle** (1994). I moved up pretty quickly. Bob, Scotty →

BOOGIE NIGHTS

While **Boogie Nights** got away with showing plenty of nudity, the Motion Picture Association of America balked at the sight of Mark Wahlberg's "clenching butt cheeks" in Dirk Diggler's first sex scene with Amber Waves (Julianne Moore), as Tichenor recalls. He and Paul Thomas Anderson trimmed the sequence by a number of frames and sent it back to the MPAA for approval—a process that repeated itself until the latter was satisfied.

MAGNOLIA

One of the most audacious sequences in **Magnolia** is the "Wise Up" number, in which all the principal characters join Aimee Mann in song. Each actor was given about a third of the song to sing, and the individual performances were then spliced together. Rather than employing dissolves, the sequence consists of a series of direct cuts from one singer to the next, lending a boldly realist texture to this most dreamlike of musical interludes.

THE ASSASSINATION OF JESSE JAMES
BY THE COWARD ROBERT FORD

The languorous pacing of Andrew Dominik's
**The Assassination of Jesse James by the Coward
Robert Ford** extends even to the climactic killing, a
tableau drawn out with an almost agonizing deliberation
as Tichenor cuts among the three men in the scene as
they slowly move into position: James (Brad Pitt) walking
over to contemplate and adjust a painting on the wall;
Ford (Casey Affleck) mustering his nerve; and Ford's
brother, Charley (Sam Rockwell), sadly looking on.

> **"My job is to be a surrogate audience, and sometimes that necessitates trimming scenes or taking them out altogether."**

and Gerri were open to my doing anything, and they let me rise to the level I was capable of. If I could do it, they said, "Go ahead, let Dylan try."

I remember Gerri cutting a scene in **The Player**, where Tim Robbins discovers someone's put a snake in his Range Rover and starts weaving all over the road. (It was an "action sequence" for Altman.) Gerri was really frustrated with the footage, which was very difficult to put together, and she wasn't achieving the sort of vibe she wanted. She just slid her chair back and said, "Get up here and do something. Change it, trim it, just fucking do something." So I did something. I don't even remember if it was good or not, and I have no idea if it made it in. Probably not. But it was great that they were training people and helping them feel confident about learning the skills.

Boogie Nights was my first feature, and I was still learning—by leaps and bounds, I was learning on that movie. Paul Thomas Anderson was also learning. Paul's a true cinematic genius, and he had all this vision and all these ideas, and in the cutting room, we felt totally free to fix and reinvent as we went along. New Line gave us enough time to work on it and make it as good as we possibly could.

The obvious challenge with **Magnolia** was to maintain the emotional pitch and not lose momentum while wading through a very long, multifaceted story. A lot of the structure was on the page, but a lot of it wasn't. I applied some of the lessons I had learned on **Short Cuts** from Gerri, who was just brilliant at making emotional connections and turning them into rhythms. Once I started editing, certain connections became →

THE ROYAL TENENBAUMS
The precise design of Wes Anderson's movies extends to their editing rhythms, as Tichenor discovered while cutting **The Royal Tenenbaums**. In certain key sequences, Anderson asked that all the shots last the same length of time. "Wes is very mathematical," Tichenor says. "Film is action over time, so in a way, mathematics, just as it applies to music, also applies to film."

> "A performance can be saved in editing, but it can also be ruined in editing. There's always the opportunity, certainly and maybe mostly in editing, to make things better or worse."

obvious, and it became clear to me that a scene would be more effective if it came after another, for instance. I do that with every movie, of course, but on a movie with so many characters and storylines, it becomes about shaping and shaping and shaping the material until you, the viewer, feel your attention isn't flagging. I don't know if we fully achieved that in **Magnolia**, but that's the kind of movie Paul wanted to make—a sort of odyssey that leaves you feeling that you've been on this wrenching journey. You could tell the same story much more economically in terms of beats and information, but at the risk of sacrificing depth of experience.

In **Magnolia**, **There Will Be Blood**, and **The Assassination of Jesse James by the Coward Robert Ford**, there are these lingering moments in which the audience is allowed to sink further into a zone. We're holding the reins loosely and letting their minds wander a bit. It can be very dangerous to let the mind wander, because you risk sacrificing chunks of your audience; it can also be very effective. You have to be very careful when doing that. Art should be made, no question; there should be room for that in American cinema. Not every film should be **Spider-Man**, **Iron Man**, or **Transformers**. But you can go too far in the other direction if you slow the pace to the point where the motion of ideas is stopping, and as an editor, I never like to do that. My job is to be a surrogate audience, and sometimes that necessitates trimming scenes or taking them out altogether. Of course, it's the director's job to push back at me and say,

THERE WILL BE BLOOD

There Will Be Blood is marked by a number of long takes, particularly this mesmerizing sequence in which Eli Sunday (Paul Dano) showily casts out a demon from a woman in his congregation. The scene is viewed from the perspective of Daniel Plainview (Daniel Day-Lewis), something we realize when the film cuts to Plainview in the doorway, observing this spectacle with the skepticism of a literal and symbolic outsider.

"No, this is going to be good." Other times the director will push back the opposite way and say, "Faster, Dylan, what are you doing?" That's why it's good to have two people involved. Something pretty funny happened about three or four years ago, actually—Paul was watching **Magnolia** on TV, and afterward he sent me a text: "Great, Dylan, **Magnolia** is too long. Thanks a lot."

Brokeback Mountain may be elegiac and dialogue-heavy, but the motion of ideas in the movie isn't slow. There's a big difference. If there's a changing perspective or a new piece of information, you don't have to be cutting fast or whiz-banging around. Ang Lee is just a master, and he's amazingly focused on story. He's got a style all his own. He could sit next to me for 30 minutes and not say anything, and just watch me work, and just his vibes flowing over me would probably influence what I was doing.

We had this lengthy conversation on **Brokeback Mountain** about these interstitial shots of running water, two or three of which I had flipped so that the water ran from left to right. Ang said, "Did you flip those shots?" I said yes, because left to right suggests time passing, and he said, "Oh, for me, right to left feels like time passing"—because, of course, Chinese lettering reads from right to left. We agreed to split the shots, so half of them would go from left to right, and the other half would go right to left.

When I'm watching dailies, I always try to look for unexpected depth in a moment or a character, something that surprises me or grabs my attention. It's usually not what the scene is →

Tichenor's thoughts on...

Art vs Cuisinart: "I really like editing to be coherent. You don't want the audience to be too disoriented. If the style is too Cuisinart, if I can't follow enough of what's happening to worry about what might happen, then as an audience member, I just lean back in my seat and sort of glaze over."

Lowered expectations: "Nowadays, of course, people will accept a lot of B.S. The editor can just line up the shots, one after another, and make sure none of them is longer than a foot, and the audience will go, 'Wow, wow, wow.' Editors like Chris Rouse and Stuart Baird don't do that; they know how to hold an audience's attention. They make sure that with the smallest bit of film, you're seeing an image or getting a piece of sound that gives your brain the clue it needs to orient itself."

The flow of ideas: "The key is to build ideas, one quick beat at a time. You see the car go around the corner, you see the car miss another car, you see the tire bump over the pothole. We're using building blocks more than we are painting a picture, which is a different approach from that of a dialogue-driven scene."

BROKEBACK MOUNTAIN

The quiet devastation of Jack Twist's death in **Brokeback Mountain** is conveyed largely through editing. As Jack's widow, Lureen (Anne Hathaway), tells Ennis Del Mar (Heath Ledger) that Jack died in an accident, Ennis envisions a darker, more truthful version of events: In contrast to the long, steady back-and-forth shots of Lureen and Ennis on the phone, the images of Jack being set upon are captured in a flurry of quick, violent cuts, rendered with an absence of sound that speaks volumes.

explicitly about. It can be tiny—three frames of just a little twitch of an ear—but those things really add up. Most moviegoers and even filmmakers are probably none the wiser, but editors are looking frame by frame. We know the difference between one frame more and one frame less. If I let the blink finish, it feels like one thing. If I stop the blink in the middle, it feels like another. It's not going to make or break a film, but those little nuances can result in an audience being much more invested in a character.

Some actors give you take one, beginning to end—and you think, wow, that was good. Take three, beginning to end, hey, that was great. Other actors give you takes one to seven, all with different ideas, and there are bits in each one to choose from. Sometimes it doesn't work—a lot of the time, when I've put together my first pass, I can wind up with a Frankenstein-feeling performance, and I then I have to scale back and decide what's important and work on it.

A performance can be saved in editing, but it can also be ruined in editing. There's always the opportunity, certainly and maybe mostly in

editing, to make things better or worse. You can have a performance that looks pretty uneven and uninteresting in dailies, and you can make it even and interesting through editing. But then there are actors who give you gold, and you're actually going to mess it up if you try to mix and match too much. Daniel Day-Lewis is one of those rare actors who is so committed, so talented, that it is very, very rare to get a false moment from him. Acting is really hard and everybody's off their rhythm on occasion, but in **There Will Be Blood**, Daniel was so consistently impressive. He was living the character and you see it onscreen. There are not too many actors who can do that.

I screen dailies the way I grew up screening dailies, and I make very, very specific notes. These days I tend to project dailies digitally in the cutting room, because nobody else watches them anymore. But I watch them that way because I want to have that feeling in a dark room, watching it on a screen, looking into the actors' eyes and really feeling the moments. That's the most important part of my job.

It's a different world now. I try to go out of my way to teach my assistants some of the things I know. But they're not getting the same broad understanding of film sound, film cutting, and film rhythm. I know I sound like an old fuddy-duddy, but when I started working in film, we had rewinds. We used gang synchronizers, grease pencils, trim bins, and Moviolas. The lab would send us thousand-foot rolls of film that we would cut with razor blades, and we had to wind all the way down through a roll of film and scan through all the footage to find something.

You don't have to do that anymore. You just jump from point to point, and it changes the way your brain works a little bit. It's hard to teach rhythm and sensitivity, but I think you learned it better in the old days, when you had to sit next to the editor and go through it together. I try to watch footage with my assistants and give them scenes to cut and bounce ideas off them. I probably don't do it as much as I should, but I do it more than most other people. It's not built into the system anymore, the way it used to be.

You had to be more certain of your ideas in the old days. You had to think it through and have a fundamental point of view about what you were trying to accomplish. Now, with computers, there's a lot less of that. Nonlinear editing is a huge, tremendous change in our industry and a boon, and it enables us to try many different things and save different versions. But I think some skill and focus can be lost with that freedom. It doesn't encourage deep thinking; it encourages shallow thinking. Because time is less precious, we are more cavalier with it. You can slap some shit together overnight, and some people will be none the wiser.

Tim Squyres

"Sometimes you have to cut because somebody blew a line or you have to switch takes, but you always want a cut to look as if you did it for a reason, rather than to hide a mistake. Every cut should have some motivation behind it, as if it's conveying some new information."

Born in 1959 in Wenonah, New Jersey, Tim Squyres first became interested in filmmaking during his undergraduate days at Cornell University. He developed experience as a director, cinematographer, editor and sound editor on various productions in Ithaca and in New York City before he was hired to cut his first feature, Marc Levin's **Blowback**, in 1989. The first assistant director on that production was Ted Hope, who with James Schamus went on to found the independent production/sales outfit Good Machine. As Squyres recalls, "When Ang Lee went to Ted and James for his first film, **Pushing Hands** (1992), Ted said, 'Oh, I know an editor who might work for cheap,' and that was me." Squyres has since edited ten of Lee's 11 features, one of which, **Crouching Tiger, Hidden Dragon** (2000), earned him an Academy Award nomination for best editing. His other editing credits include **Gosford Park** (2001, Robert Altman), **Syriana** (2005, Stephen Gaghan) and **Rachel Getting Married** (2008, Jonathan Demme). He is currently at work on **Life of Pi** (2012), Lee's twelfth feature and his first to be shot in 3D.

Tim Squyres

" Early on I realized that film editing was one of the best jobs in showbiz, because there are very few jobs, aside from writer or director, where you're involved in telling the whole story. During production, everyone does his or her part and passes it on, and then it all gets shot and comes to me. I don't mean to downplay everyone else's contributions; I can't control what people are wearing or how a scene was lit. But I like being at the end of the assembly line. Nobody can change what I've done. Nobody can fix my mistakes. I like being the last man out.

I started using the Avid very, very early, in 1992. **The Wedding Banquet** (1993) was one of the first films ever cut on the Avid. (I use the term "Avid" interchangeably with digital editing. It could be FinalCut, but the Avid is what I've always used.) People complain, or used to complain, that you lose the feel of the film when editing digitally, which to me is nonsense. Yes, it was great to be able to handle the film and use a splicer—that's a good tool, but it's not filmmaking. Filmmaking involves picture and sound, and you have better access to picture and sound in the computer than you do on film. That's truer now than it used to be.

You also had to be a bit more timid on film, because cuts had consequences. Now, if you're

SENSE AND SENSIBILITY

Far from being staid in its rhythms, **Sense and Sensibility** (1995) favored a quick cutting style in order to capture different characters' reactions to dialogue, as in this sequence, which transitions from a wide shot to sequential closeups of Gemma Jones, Harriet Walter, Hugh Grant and Emma Thompson. "Hopefully it doesn't feel fast because every shot is giving you a new piece of information," Squyres says. "If you were in the room, your head would be swinging back and forth, because you'd be interested in seeing what each person thinks."

not disciplined, you can just start cutting and cutting and cutting, without any focus, and not really get anywhere. Digital editing gives you enormous freedom, but it also requires self-discipline, and that's where people get into trouble. If you can exercise some discipline with that freedom, you will get a good result, but you'll get there having tried many other things that, if you were editing on film, you would have rejected without actually trying. Very often, the director will suggest something and you'll think, "Well, that's a terrible idea." And if you're cutting on film, and it's a big idea that requires major restructuring, you'll have to talk about it with →

Western rides again

A flop on its release in 1999, Ang Lee's Civil War drama **Ride with the Devil** was re-released in April 2010 in a director's cut that restored some 13 minutes to the original theatrical version.

Devil of a time: "The recut is something we always wanted to do," says Squyres, noting that **Ride with the Devil** was made at Universal at a time when the studio had weathered a number of expensive flops. "There was a lot of pressure on us to make the film shorter, shorter, shorter. By the time we finished the film, the people who had gotten the film made were no longer at Universal, and it was essentially Seagram's accountants making the decisions at that point."

A longer respite: One of Squyres' most significant changes was to restore a scene between two violent set-pieces near the beginning of the film. In the scene in question, Jake Roedel (Tobey Maguire) speaks to the woman who owns the house where they've taken refuge; she tells him about her son, who has lost a leg and is hiding in the barn, and whom Jake and his friend Jack Bull Chiles (Skeet Ulrich) visit. "It's tense, and it's a little bit funny, and it gives us some information about the war," Squyres says. "But most importantly, it puts more time on the clock between that first shootout at the storehouse and the big shootout in the house. That's really important because otherwise, it's just a very brief, inconsequential pause before they start shooting again."

Changing their tune: The filmmakers made some musical adjustments to the scene of the men's departure from Lawrence, right after the violent raid that results in more than 180 deaths. "The original music was too exciting, so we changed it to something that more clearly acknowledged that the raid was a bad thing," Squyres says. "It was a little too triumphant, which we had never felt good about."

> ## "Very often, the director will suggest something and you'll think, 'Well, that's a terrible idea.'"

the director at length before you try it, which can make it very hard to move forward. But with the Avid, I can just go ahead and do it anyway, and say, "See, that's why it's a terrible idea." Or maybe I'm not so smart after all, and maybe it is a good idea. Or maybe it wasn't a good idea, but it leads you to something that is.

Generally, editors don't observe how other editors work (except perhaps in television), but I get the impression that I prepare many more versions of scenes than most editors do. I tend to give the director three versions of something the first day; new directors tend to be surprised by that. And then there are usually a few more alternatives I haven't even shown them. My job is to explore the footage, and prepare myself in terms of my own knowledge of the footage, so

that when the director wants to try something else, either I've already done it, or I can do it quickly and easily. I try to work with the footage for a while, rather than just come up with a plan beforehand and execute the plan, because I've generally worked with directors who don't give me a plan. Ang Lee has never told me, "Here's how the scene is supposed to be cut." I always tell directors that I'm happy to take any direction they want to give me, but I'm not going to limit myself to that, because then I wouldn't be doing my job.

Ang and I work together so well because we disagree just enough. He once told somebody that we disagree all the time, and I said, "No, we agree 95 percent of the time. It's just that the last five percent is all we talk about." Our aesthetics

CROUCHING TIGER, HIDDEN DRAGON
Most of the fight scenes in **Crouching Tiger, Hidden Dragon** were shot without sound, or MOS ("mit out sound"). Rather than apply sound effects for every grunt, kick and clanging sword, which would have taxed the low-budget production's resources, Squyres (who also served as the film's music editor) spent considerable time finding the right musical accompaniment for each action sequence.

For the first martial-arts sequence, an over-the-rooftops chase culminating in a battle between Michelle Yeoh and Zhang Ziyi, Squyres used a temp track consisting of Japanese taiko drumming. "When we screened the assembly, my assistant was in the back operating the volume knob, and I said, 'Just keep inching it up during the scene, and by the end, I want it loud.' Nobody ever considered a different musical approach."

are similar enough that it's never a stretch for me to understand what he's doing in a film. I've never had to figure out what Ang was up to. He does occasionally push me to do things I wouldn't do, and I push him to do things he wouldn't do. Ideally, you push each other enough that the film you wind up making is better than the film that either of you would have made on your own. It's a very healthy relationship, and that's why you often see editors and directors working together over and over again. When you have a system that works, you tend to stick with it.

It really hit me on **Sense and Sensibility** (1995) that one of the most important aspects of the editor's job is to deal with performance. Many approach editing as a technical job, but the most important thing I did on that movie was to look at something Emma Thompson had done, and then look at another take, and say, "Hmm, that's not good." Not only am I allowed to say that, but it's my job to say that. I'm required to pass judgment on these tremendous performances. It's a very emotional job. You have to experience the emotions that are inherent in the scene and believe in them, and you try to keep that day after day and bring out the best in those performances, which is a very different job from simply matching the head turns and keeping the tempo fast. The heart of the job is really about performance, and I think if you ask most editors what scene they're proudest of, it won't be an action scene. It'll be an emotional, dialogue-driven scene. Those are always the biggest challenge. →

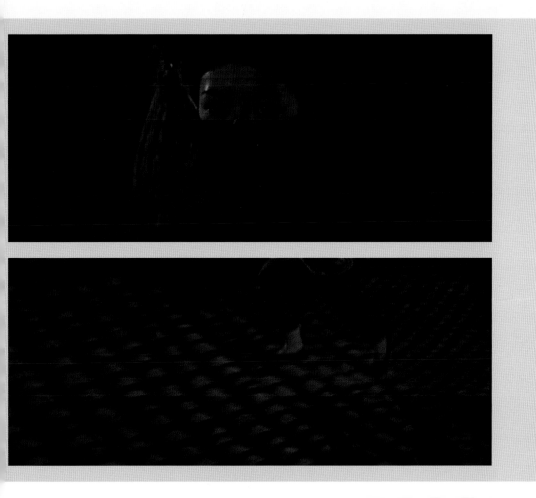

"Assembling a martial-arts film isn't even a full-time job; they would spend two weeks shooting an action scene, which I would cut in four days."

In **Sense and Sensibility**, the characters are all keeping secrets from each other, so when one character says something, it means one thing to this person and something else to that person. If you were in the room, your head would be swinging back and forth, because you'd be interested in seeing what each person thinks. In a scene like that, there's an awful lot you want to look at, so you're never at a loss for where to cut to. Sometimes you have to cut because somebody blew a line or you have to switch takes, but you always want a cut to look as if you did it for a reason, rather than to hide a mistake. Every cut should have some motivation behind it, as if it's conveying some new information. So in a film like **Sense and Sensibility**, there's always some place to go, because those scenes

are so rich emotionally and thematically. There's so much that you want to cover, and if you look at that film, some scenes are cut very, very fast— hopefully not in an annoying way, because every shot is showing you something new.

A film like **The Ice Storm**, **Gosford Park** or **Syriana** is much more challenging, because a major part of the job is rearranging scenes rather than cutting the scenes themselves, in which case you can expect to add a month or two to post-production. **The Ice Storm** (1997) was hard. It isn't plot-driven; it's relatively unstructured and contains several interlocking stories. And because the film was written to be kind of a satire and directed to be more of a drama, much of the tone had to be discovered in the editing room. It's probably the most significantly restructured film I've worked on with Ang. No

EAT DRINK MAN WOMAN
Ang Lee spent five days shooting the five-minute dinner preparation montage that opens **Eat Drink Man Woman**, a luscious sequence in which fish are fried, dumplings are folded and viewers' appetites are whetted. "James Schamus said, 'Tim, you've got to tell him to stop,'" Squyres recalls. "And I said, 'No, this is great!' What's so crucial about that sequence is at the end of it, you're thinking, 'I'm going to like this movie.' Plus we bought enough goodwill to get us through the next ten minutes, which are the weakest part of the movie."

剪接：李 安
Tim Squyres

SYRIANA

Squyres felt free to break the rules in **Syriana**, following the lead of Robert Elswit's darting camerawork and the deliberately fractured nature of the material. These techniques are apparent even in this simple scene between Matt Damon and Amanda Peet, which is never presented from the same angle twice. "We jumped the line all over the place, and I made a point of trying not to go back to a matching eyeline. I never wanted to go back to the same shot that I left," he says.

one could ever agree on what worked and what didn't, or how to fix it. By the end of **Sense and Sensibility**, we had gotten to a point where we felt very good about the final cut; with **The Ice Storm**, we never got there. Eventually, it just came time to stop. For years I couldn't watch the film, but after about five years I saw it again, and I was able to see it for what it was, and I thought, "Hey, this movie's pretty good." Still, it's funny when people tell me, "That movie seems so perfectly realized, as if it was designed that way." I just kind of smile and laugh and say, "Thank you."

When Ang told me he was doing a martial-arts film (**Crouching Tiger, Hidden Dragon**), I was astonished. But it was an exciting project, and we were very much on the same page throughout. We talked beforehand about what we liked and didn't like about martial-arts movies. The fight choreography, the shooting and the editing were all designed to be fluid and smooth; we didn't want it to feel too abrupt or jagged. The funny thing is, I received an Oscar nomination for that film, and I suspect that was because of the action

scenes, but in a way, that was the easy part. Assembling a martial-arts film isn't even a full-time job; they would spend two weeks shooting an action scene, which I would cut in four days. We had to cut all the fight scenes first, because of all the wire removals, and then we spent the rest of the time doing the hard part, which was the dialogue. Some of those scenes we just beat to death, in part because the scripts I received had been translated very poorly from the original Chinese, to the point of being virtually incomprehensible. I was really going on faith that it all made sense. If it hadn't been Ang, I wouldn't have done it.

Gosford Park (2001) was a real treat. To have the opportunity to cut one of Robert Altman's movies—he was one of the directors who inspired me to go into filmmaking—was quite a thrill. It was a complicated movie, given the cast and the length of the script, and he didn't shoot normal coverage at all. He actually had a shockingly small amount of footage for that film, and a lot of my usual procedures didn't work →

> "As an editor, it's very important that you don't develop your own personal style. Your style has to be informed by the footage."

because of the way he shot it. The cameras were always moving, and he would just dolly them back and forth, with no plan whatsoever. The editing was really about just looking at the footage and finding the moments that worked. Usually, if you like take seven better than take four, you can just swap them, but not in Gosford Park, because the camera was someplace different and so the cuts didn't match up anymore. You couldn't just mix and match. Each scene was a very complicated little puzzle, on top of the larger puzzle of cutting back and forth among several different stories upstairs and downstairs.

Bob is a director in the most literal sense, in that he takes what everyone brings to the project and directs it all so that everyone's working together. But he doesn't tell you what to do. He wants to see what you bring to it, and then he'll nudge it in a certain direction so that it's working with what everyone else is bringing to the scene. And in the end, **Gosford Park** was meant to be a little bit messy in terms of its visual style. Bob didn't want to make it easy. It's supposed to be a little bit challenging and complicated. It took me a while to figure out his aesthetic; I had seen a lot of his movies, but that's very different from actually internalizing it and cutting the film in a manner that's Altmanesque.

If I had done **Rachel Getting Married** (2008) before **Gosford Park**, I would have had a much harder time with it. **Rachel Getting Married** is an incredibly loose, improvisational film, and it was shot almost like a documentary. The wedding rehearsal scene was done in two 45-minute takes with five cameras, and that was it. Jonathan Demme wanted people to experiment, and he wanted me to experiment, and there were so many different ways to cut

LUST, CAUTION

The opening scene of four women playing mahjong in **Lust, Caution** (2007) required at least 70 setups and took more than a week to shoot. To simplify the problem of whittling down nearly eight hours of footage into a three-and-a-half-minute scene that retained the nuance in every glance and gesture, Squyres established a main eyeline between the two main characters in the scene (played by Tang Wei and Joan Chen). He then cut

several different versions of the sequence—two on either side of the eyeline, one in wide shots only, one in closeups only—in order to isolate and extract the best pieces. "I really beat that scene to death," Squyres recalls. "By the end I felt I had tried everything I wanted to try, through this painstaking process of taking it apart piece by piece and then synthesizing it into a cut that utilizes everything."

that footage. When you have footage like that, just knowing what to do with it is difficult. You don't have the sort of structural crutches you normally have, such as medium shots, closeups and matching eyelines.

In the wedding rehearsal scene, Anne Hathaway gets up and makes this toast, which is just about one of the most awkward moments in cinema history. Normally, that would have been the end of that scene and we would have cut away. But we didn't do that. We went on, and three more people gave toasts before we left that scene. We liked the idea of saying that in real life, there are no scene cuts. People in a situation like that would overcome that awkwardness, and just get on with the evening. Jonathan wanted it to be kind of messy and indulgent, but in a good way.

As an editor, it's very important that you don't develop your own personal style. Your style has to be informed by the footage. And so the style I used on **Rachel Getting Married** is very different from the style I used on **Sense and Sensibility**. They're different films, and it's important to be flexible and sensitive to what the strengths of the footage are and what's right for the project. I'm really happy not to have to keep cutting the same film over and over again. "

Valdís Óskarsdóttir

"When I'm editing, I'm not in this world; I'm
in the world of the film and the story that I'm
telling. If I'm constantly being interrupted, I can't
concentrate. When people are telling you what
to do all the time, your brain stops working."

Born in Akureyri, Iceland, and raised in Reykjavik, Valdís Óskarsdóttir landed her first film gigs as an assistant for local directors such as Thráinn Bertelsson and Fridrik Thor Fridriksson. After studying at the National Film School of Denmark in Copenhagen for four years, during which she spent her summers cutting news broadcasts for Icelandic television, Óskarsdóttir received her first feature editing credits on Ásdís Thoroddsen's **Ingaló** (1992) and Óskar Jónasson's **Sódóma Reykjavik** (1992).

Her international breakthrough came with Danish director Thomas Vinterberg's **The Celebration** (1998), the first film to be produced under the rules of the Dogme 95 manifesto. She edited two more Dogme films, Søren Kragh-Jacobsen's **Mifune's** (1999) and Harmony Korine's **Julien Donkey-Boy** (1999), and soon after made her Hollywood debut working on Gus Van Sant's **Finding Forrester** (2000). Óskarsdóttir won the BAFTA Award for best editing, an ACE Eddie Award nomination and numerous other prizes for her work on Michel Gondry's **Eternal Sunshine of the Spotless Mind** (2004). Her other editing credits include Sergey Bodrov's **Mongol: The Rise to Power of Genghis Khan** (2007) and Vinterberg's **Submarino** (2010), as well as two Icelandic features that she also wrote and directed, **Country Wedding** (2008) and **King's Road** (2010).

Valdís Óskarsdóttir

When I sat down in front of a Steenbeck for the first time, during a filmmaking seminar in Stockholm in 1984, I knew I had found what I wanted to do for the rest of my life. When I got back to Iceland, I talked to everyone in the film business and asked if I could get a job as an editor. But they always said, "No, we just do it ourselves." So I decided to forget all about film editing and got a job as a newspaper photographer. I had been working for a week when I got a phone call from Thráinn Bertelsson, who offered me a job on his upcoming film as a clapper loader and still photographer. I said yes without hesitation. After the shoot, I worked as an assistant editor and assistant sound editor on the film. I assisted on a few films after that, but I knew that if I was serious, I would have to go abroad to learn how to edit. There were no such opportunities in Iceland.

The turning point came when I went to see **Amadeus**. I remember emerging from the cinema and saying to myself, "I'm never going to be like this Salieri guy." I was determined not to become jealous and frustrated in life. At the encouragement of Tómas Gíslason, the editor I had worked with, I applied to the National Film School of Denmark in 1987 and was accepted. I totally ignored the fact that I was a single mother with two kids and moved to Copenhagen for four years.

While I was at school, Tómas conducted a series of interviews with top film editors in the States. I got to cut the footage with three other students on the editing line, and I was lucky enough to get Dede Allen. She became my mentor. I learned more editing her interview than I did during my four years of school. Film schools can teach you technique, but they can't teach you pacing and rhythm; those are things you have to have in you to begin with, or you have to teach and train yourself. Everything Dede said, I took in. She taught me never to use music while I was editing, because if I could make a scene work without music, it would work perfectly with music. She taught me that editing action is fun, but editing dialogue is difficult, so I studied in detail how she cut dialogue.

Another thing I learned from Dede was to never do assembly of scenes and to pick the best performances right from the beginning. "Because how do you know if a scene works if you don't do it properly?" she said. She was right. The first time I sat down to edit a feature, I was so overwhelmed thinking about how much material I had to work with. So as not to have a nervous breakdown, I just started with one scene, finished it, and then took the next scene and finished that. I still work like that. I never got to meet Dede,

THE CELEBRATION

The first film produced under the Dogme 95 manifesto, Thomas Vinterberg's **The Celebration** required Valdís Óskarsdóttir to obey certain rules but allowed her to break many more. One of the film's most potent scenes, in which Christian (Ulrich Thomsen) stands up to deliver an altogether surprising toast at the birthday party of his father (Henning Moritzen), derives much of its tension from Óskarsdóttir's use of rapid cuts to continually frame and reframe the action from different angles. The result lends the proceedings the distinct sense of having been captured on the fly, while also making the viewer feel like a party guest with the best seat in the house.

which is a shame. I never had the opportunity to thank her for what she did for me.

Because **The Celebration** (1998) was a Dogme 95 film, I had to read the rules of what I could and couldn't do in editing. I could only do straight cuts; I couldn't use sound from one take and lay it over another take; and I couldn't use music at all unless it had been recorded in the shot. All that aside, it was remarkably freeing. Here was something totally new, and I felt I could do whatever I wanted in the editing. I could cross the line, cut back and forth on a camera movement, and use jump cuts. In fact, my approach to every scene was to ask myself what I would ordinarily do, and then do the opposite. It was probably hard work, but to me it was a game and I loved it.

Thomas Vinterberg shot about 56 hours of material on **The Celebration**, with each scene covered by two to six cameras, and I had to watch every take separately to find what I was looking for. It took time, but it wasn't too difficult. The script was very tight, and nothing was improvised, which made it much easier. Even still, we stripped it down; there were many scenes that we had to trim, rearrange or take out altogether. We even ended up eliminating one character entirely. It always came down to what

was the best way to tell the story, and if there was something that wasn't serving the narrative, we cut it out.

Thomas and I have worked together now since 1995. We've been through hell together and we've been through heaven together. We're very fond of each other, and we can talk and argue all we like and still be best friends. It took a couple of films, though, for me to teach him how to behave in a cutting room. After I finished the first cut of **The Celebration**, Thomas would sit by my side in front of the Avid, and often he would tell me what to do and how to do it. It's very tiresome and annoying when directors do that. I have nothing against the director being in the room, so long as he keeps quiet while I'm working. When I'm editing, I'm not in this world; I'm in the world of the film and the story that I'm telling. If I'm constantly being interrupted, I can't concentrate. When people are telling you what to do all the time, your brain stops working.

I had a similar problem at first with Søren Kragh-Jacobsen on **Mifune** (1999). He would sit in the corner of the cutting room all day long, and he talked a lot. Also, he would snap his fingers every time he said, "Cut!" It became really irritating because he did that on every cut I made. Finally, at one point, I stopped working →

MIFUNE

The Dogme 95 romantic comedy **Mifune** originally opened by cross-cutting between its two romantic leads, a strategy that Óskarsdóttir and director Søren Kragh-Jacobsen ended up scrapping completely in the cutting room. In the new and final version, the parallel stories of Kresten (Anders W. Berthelsen) and Liva (Iben Hjejle) unfold one after the other, with no intercutting. Óskarsdóttir recalls that they were only fussing with the film at the time because their computer had crashed a few days before. Had it not been for that malfunction, the film would have gone unchanged. "I guess it was meant to be," she says.

Danmarks Radio/Nimbus

and said, "If you snap your fingers one more time, I'm going to bite you in the leg." And he said, "Really?" "Yes," I said, "if your trousers are clean." So he taped two of his fingers together so he couldn't snap them anymore. After that, we were fine.

Mifune ended up being quite different from what we had initially planned. Originally, the opening scenes had cross-cut between the guy, Kresten, and the girl, Liva, before their eventual meeting. The day before we were supposed to deliver the film to the lab, Søren and I were watching it one last time to make sure everything was all right. Twenty minutes into the film, we got a call from someone associated with the film, and he said, "Instead of cross-cutting between Kresten and Liva, have you ever thought of just telling his story first and then her story?" We were supposed to have a locked picture the next

day, but Søren and I just looked at each other, and I said, "I like this idea. Let's do it." And we did it.

I had a lot of fun cutting **Julien Donkey-Boy** (1999) for Harmony Korine. All the dialogue was improvised except for one scene, and there were cameras all over the place. I had enormous freedom in the cutting room. Harmony never interfered. He dropped by maybe once or twice a week to see what I had done, and he would say, "Great," and just go home. It wasn't until I had finished everything that we sat down together and decided what to take out or leave in. We decided that the style should be very fragmented, so that the viewer would never know what to expect or what the next scene would bring.

Anthony Dod Mantle and Harmony shot a lot of extra material, and there were many scenes that should have been kept in. Some scenes ran

Dogme 95

Dogme 95 is an avant-garde filmmaking movement set up by Danish directors Lars von Trier and Thomas Winterberg. The Manifesto they put together outlined a genre of filmmaking based on traditional values of story, acting and theme, returning to a simple approach rather than employing the means of elaborate visual effects, post-production modifications and technological gimmickry. Von Trier and Winterberg announced the rules for the Dogme 95 on March 22, 1995, in Paris, at the *Le cinéma vers son deuxième siècle conference*, to an audience gathered to celebrate the first 100 years of film, and to discuss its future. The Manifesto was set out as follows:

- Filming must be done on location. Props and sets must not be brought in. If a particular prop is necessary for a story, a location must be chosen where this prop is to be found.
- The sound must never be produced apart from the images or vice versa. Music must not be used unless it occurs within the scene being filmed, i.e. diegetic
- The camera must be a handheld camera. Any movement or immobility attainable in the hand is permitted. The film must not take place where the camera is standing; filming must take place where the action takes place.
- The film must be in color. Special lighting is not acceptable (if there is too little light for exposure the scene must be cut or a single lamp be attached to the camera).
- Optical work and filters are forbidden.
- The film must not contain superficial action (murder, weapons, etc. must not occur).
- Temporal and geographical alienation are forbidden (that is to say that the film takes place here and now).
- Genre movies are not acceptable.
- The film format must be Academy 35mm.
- The director must not be credited.

very, very long, and it was impossible to trim them down, so we had to take them out. If you're trying to maintain a certain rhythm and suddenly you throw in a seven-minute dialogue scene, the whole thing just collapses. But it was heartbreaking to take out some of those scenes, especially since Ewen Bremner gave such a great performance as Julien. I felt very sorry for Julien. I've always wanted to sit down and cut another version of **Julien Donkey-Boy**, and restore all the scenes we took out. It's the only film I've done that I would like to recut.

Finding Forrester (2000) was my first "big" film, so to speak. But for me, it was just another editing job. Sure, it was a different kind of story, shot in a different way, but my method of editing is always the same—I just tell the story. Gus Van Sant was wonderful to work with. Once, during shooting, I asked him if there was something special he wanted me to do on a particular scene, and he said, "You're the editor. You edit the film." When we started working on the director's cut, he was in the cutting room every day, but he never talked while I was working. He just sat there, working on his computer or playing his guitar. If I stopped working, he would offer a comment if he had one, and I could ask him what he thought if I wasn't sure I was doing the right thing. He was always there if I needed him. I'm not sure there are many directors who can do that.

I spent about nine months editing **Eternal Sunshine of the Spotless Mind** (2004), which was a very difficult project. Sometimes you work on films that give you so much back, you can keep up your energy. **Eternal Sunshine of the Spotless Mind** was that kind of a film and I guess it shows onscreen. And sometimes you work on films that just suck everything out of you, and →

ETERNAL SUNSHINE OF THE SPOTLESS MIND

When working together on **Eternal Sunshine of the Spotless Mind**, director Michel Gondry and Óskarsdóttir agreed that they didn't want Jim Carrey to retain any of his trademark comedic mannerisms in the film. "I thought of him in **The Truman Show**, which showed he was capable of doing something different," Óskarsdóttir says. "So that's what I looked for in the material, moments where he was nothing like Jim Carrey."

JULIEN DONKEY-BOY

For **Julien Donkey-Boy**, director Harmony Korine and Óskarsdóttir favored a fragmentary, time-shuffling editorial approach designed to keep the viewer consistently off balance. Korine and cinematographer Anthony Dod Mantle shot a great deal of extra material, much of which Óskarsdóttir had to leave out, to her regret. While these cuts helped maintain the picture's rhythm, they came at the cost of considerable insight into the central character of Julien (Ewen Bremner). "I felt very sorry for Julien," Óskarsdóttir says. "It's the only film I've done that I would like to recut."

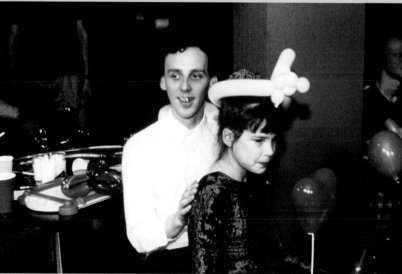

The next generation

One of the more significant casualties of digital editing has been the built-in system of apprenticeship that once thrived in the days of mechanical cutting, allowing an eager young assistant editor to move up the ladder in a relatively short time. Still, mentorship and encouragement continue: Óskarsdóttir worked closely and bonded with two additional editors on **Eternal Sunshine of the Spotless Mind**, both of whom have done her proud in the years since.

Jeffrey M. Werner is the editor of the independent productions **Right at Your Door** (2006), **The Dog Problem** (2006) and **Sleep Dealer** (2008), as well as the documentaries **So Goes the Nation** (2006) and **Religulous** (2008). He received an ACE Eddie Award nomination for editing Lisa Cholodenko's **The Kids Are All Right** (2010).

Paul Zucker, who also assisted Óskarsdóttir on **Julien Donkey-Boy** and **Finding Forrester**, went on to cut Harmony Korine's **Mister Lonely**, though the higher-profile Óskarsdóttir was billed as the editor to appease some of the film's European financiers. ("I asked them if they would take my name out, but they wouldn't," Óskarsdóttir says. "I think it's a shame, because Paul did a very good job on that film.") Zucker also edited the independent pictures **Delirious** (2006), **Twelve** (2010), **Return** (2011) and **Here** (2011).

"Sometimes you work on films that give you so much back, you can keep up your energy. And sometimes you work on films that just suck everything out of you."

when you crawl out of the cutting room, closer to death than to life, you never want to cut a frame again. But that's how I tend to work; I invest everything in the film that I'm editing— my feelings, my heart and my soul. I neglect my family and my friends because the film becomes my family and my friend.

There were more than a 100 hours of material, and the first cut took a very long time. Still, in the spirit of Dede Allen, I didn't do a "quick-and-dirty assembly," but worked on each scene until I was satisfied with the outcome. Fortunately, I had the greatest editorial department ever: In addition to our post-production manager, Mike Jackman, and his team, I had two assistants, Jeff Werner and Paul Zucker (whom I had worked with on **Julien Donkey-Boy** and **Finding Forrester**, and who later went on to edit **Mister Lonely** for Harmony). Paul, Jeff and I were mostly left alone in the cutting room during the last four months. We had great support from Charlie Kaufman and our producers, Anthony Bregman and Steve Golin, and we just cut the film as we felt it wanted to be cut. I always say that I'm not

really cutting the film. The story is in the material that was shot and you just have to dig it out. The editor's role is to help the film to emerge the way it wants to, because it can't do it on its own.

Above all, we had Charlie's fantastic script and the visual genius of Michel Gondry. The film probably would not have been what it was without his vision. Michel didn't have the patience to sit in the cutting room longer than two hours at a time, and we argued a lot. He's French and I'm Icelandic, and we're both stubborn, so that might be an explanation. He was used to doing things his way and I was used to doing things my way. There were a lot of nasty words, tears and slammed doors, but also a lot of kind words, laughs and open doors. It was like riding a rollercoaster, but it was worth every minute. I don't necessarily want to do it over again, but if I had to, I would.

The film's structure was in the script, but we shortened scenes, shuffled them around and made a few changes here and there. The material made a good fit with the style I had

ETERNAL SUNSHINE OF THE SPOTLESS MIND
While an intricate story structure may seem impressive from an editing standpoint, Óskarsdóttir points out that editors often get credit for the writer's original work. While she and her team trimmed and repositioned a few scenes in **Eternal Sunshine of the Spotless Mind**, "the film's structure was in the script," she notes. "There wasn't much that you could shuffle around, especially when the story starts to go backward in time. There are a lot of things you can do in the editing room, but there's a limit."

used on **The Celebration** and **Julien Donkey-Boy**. I like that kind of editing, where you're jumping around a lot, but it has to suit the story you're telling. You would never edit **Gone with the Wind** that way, for instance, and if you tried editing **Eternal Sunshine** in the manner of **Gone with the Wind**, it would probably bore you to death. Every film has its own style. It's all about being true to the material you have to work with and making sure you don't force anything upon it. Your loyalty always lies with the characters and the story, never with the director or producers. You should treat the film like a human being.

I wouldn't call myself a director. I'm an editor first and a director second. The only reason I began directing my own films was that I had cut two films that turned out to be very bad experiences, to the point that I decided to quit editing. I think that's the worst thing you can allow anyone to do, which is to kill a passion that you have in life. I didn't know how to do anything besides filmmaking, and I had written the story of **Country Wedding** (2008), so I decided to make the film. We shot it in seven days with four

cameras. Unfortunately, the person who was supposed to edit the film couldn't do it, so I stepped in. It took nine months to edit, mostly because it was improvised, but also because I had to fight against my panic of entering the cutting room almost every single day.

Since then I've directed another film, **King's Road** (2010), and edited three feature films and a couple of shorts. Gradually I've regained the joy of editing, of creating a story and feeling that sense of freedom in front of the computer, totally lost in a world of imagination and creativity. It's the greatest escape from reality I've ever known. I plan to keep that passion in a safe place, because I don't want anyone to harm it again. 🙸

Dede Allen

Dede Allen was the first editor, male or female, to receive a solo title card on a film—a fitting distinction for someone who made a persuasive case for film editing as not merely a technical discipline, but an art worth considering in its own right. Over the course of a career that spanned nearly 20 feature films and 60 years—during which she worked with Sidney Lumet, Robert Rossen, Warren Beatty, Robert Redford and, most notably, Arthur Penn—Allen pioneered a range of bold, innovative techniques, jazzing up the relatively staid tradition of American film editing with an exciting, intuitive style inspired in large part by the formal experimentation of the French *nouvelle vague*.

The film that earned Allen that exclusive credit, Penn's **Bonnie and Clyde** (1967), is still considered her signature work, celebrated for a jagged, modernist cutting style that expressed the violence wrought by the titular duo. Many of her other key films have been informed by a similar kineticism, from the pool-hall sequences in **The Hustler** (1961) to the raw, real-time immediacy of **Dog Day Afternoon** (1975).

Born Dorothea Carruthers Allen in 1923 in Cincinnati, Allen dropped out of Scripps College to take a job as a messenger at Columbia Pictures. Working her way up, she learned the craft of editing from TV cutter Carl Lerner, but opportunities for advancement proved elusive and she eventually moved to Europe with her husband, Stephen Fleischman.

After some time abroad, she and her family moved to New York City, where she honed her craft by editing commercials. In 1959, Allen received her first editor credit for the gangster drama **Odds Against Tomorrow**, directed by Robert Wise (who himself had cut his teeth as the editor of **Citizen Kane**). But it wasn't until she edited Rossen's **The Hustler** that Allen applied and perfected her panoply of European-influenced techniques, which included such now-standard innovations as jump cutting and overlapping audio from one scene to the next (or previous).

This was followed by Elia Kazan's **America, America** (1963) and Penn's **Bonnie and Clyde**, **Alice's Restaurant** (1969), **Little Big Man** (1970), **Night Moves** (1975) and **The Missouri Breaks** (1976). Allen also edited films for the director George Roy Hill including **Slaughterhouse-Five** (1972), crucially managing the film's frequent and abrupt temporal shifts, and **Slap Shot** (1977), lending vigor to the hockey film's often violent

01 Slap Shot

02 The Hustler

sequences on the rink. Allen cut Lumet's **Serpico** (1973), **Dog Day Afternoon** and **The Wiz** (1978), as well as Warren Beatty's epic **Reds** (1981), which required her to cut down more than two million feet of film.

Her later credits included John Hughes' **The Breakfast Club** (1985); Philip Kaufman's **Henry & June** (1990); and Barry Sonnenfeld's **The Addams Family** (1991), after which she stopped editing for several years to work as an executive at Warner Bros. She returned to the cutting room for Curtis Hanson's **Wonder Boys** (2000).

Allen received Academy Award nominations for editing **Dog Day Afternoon**, **Reds** (with Craig McKay and **Wonder Boys**. She never won a competitive Oscar or ACE Eddie Award, although she did receive the latter organization's career achievement award in 1994. She died of a stroke in 2010, leaving behind her husband; her son, Tom Fleischman, a sound re-recording mixer; and her daughter, Ramey Ward. She also left behind a not insignificant number of protégés, whether they learned to edit alongside her or simply gained inspiration from her remarkably influential body of work.

03 Bonnie and Clyde

04 Reds

05 Dog Day Afternoon

Virginia Katz

"When I watch dailies, I'm looking for those little pieces—that telltale head tilt or eye movement that sticks in my brain. I try to use every little gem I can find."

Virginia Katz learned the basics of film editing from her father, the veteran editor Sidney Katz, working alongside him in his New York cutting room. After moving to Los Angeles in the 1980s, where she was mentored by Marion Rothman and edited a number of telefilms, Katz received her first feature editing credit on Bill Condon's horror-thriller **Candyman: Farewell to the Flesh** (1995). It was the first of several films she would edit for Condon, including **Gods and Monsters** (1998), **Kinsey** (2004), and **Dreamgirls** (2006), for which she won an ACE Eddie Award for best editing, comedy, or musical. She most recently edited Condon's **The Twilight Saga: Breaking Dawn**, (2011/12) the two-part finale of the popular teen-vampire franchise. Her other credits include Steve Antin's **Burlesque** (2010), Ronny Yu's **Fearless** (2006) edited with Richard Learoyd, Dan Ireland's **Mrs. Palfrey at the Claremont** (2005), and episodes of TV series such as ABC's **Alias** and the WB's **Felicity**.

Virginia Katz

"After my father retired, he'd always call me and ask, "Are you up to camera yet?" I knew he did it to get my goat because I was nowhere near up to camera, and my dad knew that. He died two years ago. I miss him very much and I miss those phone calls. I was very blessed to have a parent who led me into a career that just happened to be right for me.

It all began one summer when my parents insisted I find a job, so I started working in his cutting room. I had no idea what editing was about, but I fell in love with the process and knew pretty quickly that it was what I wanted to do. My father was a terrific teacher and a very, very patient one. Two weeks in, he handed me the dailies of a scene and said, "Cut this." The scene involved two characters talking, and when the person on the right talked, I'd cut to him. When the person on the left talked, I'd cut to her. After a while I started to see why that wouldn't quite work, and as my father kept giving me film and teaching me to play around with the sound, little by little I learned how to find the rhythm of the scene.

As an editor you have to find your own way of cutting. If you were to line up five editors, you'd get five different versions of the same scene. You eventually find your own rhythm and sense of timing, and I don't think it's something that can be taught. You figure it out instinctively.

When I was working with my father in New York we didn't have a music editor, so I would be the one to take the composer's notes and timings. We did a lot of the sound work ourselves, including making all of our ADR loops. I feel that's an important part of the process, learning all aspects of post-production.

On a TV show like **Alias**, you have about four days to assemble a first cut. The time constraint doesn't permit you to sit and meditate over every cut. You lock it two weeks later, and then it's out of your hands. You don't get the chance to swaddle the baby. I find features more challenging

GODS AND MONSTERS
This film makes playful use of black-and-white fantasy interludes that deliberately evoke the classic Frankenstein movies of James Whale (played by Sir Ian McKellen). Toward the end of Bill Condon's film, Whale begins to lose his grip on reality—a psychological conceit Katz underscored by deploying direct cuts from Whale to whatever ghostly vision he perceives, be it Frankenstein's monster or a former lover.

because there is more film and you have more time to put it together. For me, it's more rewarding. When you get to see it through from start to finish, you feel you're really contributing to the whole package. I admit, I'm a control freak and want to ensure that we have the best sound and music. I certainly don't take credit for doing any of those jobs, but like most editors, I want to be along for the whole ride.

When I moved to Los Angeles I started working as an apprentice to Marion Rothman, a fabulous editor. I enjoyed being an assistant, but when I started to feel I could do what Marion was doing I realized it was time to try and move up. The hardest thing for an aspiring editor is finding that person who will have confidence in you—who knows that although you might not have a lot of experience, you have the desire and hopefully the talent to do the job. I did have the advantage of encouragement and experience from my father, but I also had persistence and the desire

to cut—at a time, truth be told, when it wasn't easy for a woman to move up as an editor. Luck had a lot to do with it, too. I was working with Marion on **Sister, Sister** (1987), which was Bill Condon's first directing job, and I ended up doing quite a bit of cutting. Bill and I just hit it off, and I followed him onto his next film. It's been 24 years and we're still working together.

Bill is very supportive. When we are shooting I show him cut scenes, but it isn't until we are finished shooting and begin the director's cut that we can really go to work. I enjoy doing my first cut but I'm always thankful when it's time for Bill to come in. I crave the solitude of this cutting room and I'm very happy to be in here working with the door shut, but just as a director is glad to be out of the field and in the cutting room, so I'm glad to have him with me. That's when we can really start to shape the movie.

There's a great sense of freedom when you're working on an independent production like →

"My biggest reason for loving digital editing is that it's made me a calmer, nicer person."

Gods and Monsters (1998). Even though the talent involved was unbelievable, it was a low-budget movie. There wasn't a studio looming over us. It was a short shooting schedule, the performances were wonderful, and being able to take footage from James Whale's old Frankenstein movies and incorporate it into the story was just a joy. The challenge, in that case, was simply getting the best of the best, because everybody was good. Again, having ample time to go through every take is crucial, especially when you're trying to get the best performances. When I watch dailies, I'm looking for those little pieces—that telltale head tilt or eye movement that sticks in my brain. I try to use every little gem I can find. Sometimes it's hard and sometimes it isn't, depending on who the actor is. Ian McKellen could have been reading from the phone book and I would still have found these precious pieces.

I don't remember any scene with him or with Lynn Redgrave where I had to look too hard.

Dreamgirls (2006) was a much bigger challenge because there was so much more footage. I think there was nearly a million feet of film. They spent the first two weeks shooting the extended talent-show sequence at the beginning of the film. There were four cameras on all the numbers and there were just massive amounts of footage coming in. It was daunting. Under these circumstances we could have gotten a second editor, but I wanted to cut the material on my own and Bill wanted that as well.

If I were still editing on film, **Dreamgirls** would have taken two years to cut. My biggest reason for loving digital editing is that it's made me a calmer, nicer person. Physically, it's just so much simpler: You never lose film, you don't rip the film trying to feed it through the Moviola, and you

DREAMGIRLS

For the showstopping "And I Am Telling You I'm Not Going" number, Katz opted to hold Jennifer Hudson primarily in closeup, with occasional cutaways to long shots in order to convey a sense of her isolation on a big, empty stage. "There were huge amounts of film and many different takes and choices, but we stayed mainly on her because she performed so beautifully," Katz says. "It was really about her."

don't have ripped fingers from sprocket holes! And on top of that, it's so easy to make changes when you're editing digitally. Let's say I want to make a dissolve and we're editing on film. It goes to the optical house but if it doesn't work, we've spent all this money and gotten nowhere. On the Avid, you can do all that in seconds and if it doesn't work, it costs you nothing.

It's great to be able to play and experiment, to be able to move shots around and try anything and everything. I think on the Avid you get the best version of a scene that you can get, because on film you just could not have taken the time. When you think of the old days and the great epic movies, it's amazing how they managed to edit them in the time they had. It was so prehistoric. With the advances in digital technology, I can't ever imagine going back to film. It was just too burdensome. →

A fearless challenge

Never one to be pigeonholed by genre or style, Katz was up for something new when director Ronny Yu asked her to edit **Fearless**, his kinetic period drama starring Jet Li as the legendary Chinese martial artist Huo Yuanjia.

Lost in translation: Cutting a film partially or entirely in a foreign language, without the benefit of subtitles, can pose a unique challenge for an editor. The bulk of this challenge fell to Katz, who cut most of the film's dialogue-driven dramatic scenes as opposed to the relatively wordless fight sequences; fortunately, she had an assistant who could speak Chinese and translate as needed.

The language of action: "You want to make sure you see what you're supposed to see, and keep an exciting rhythm going," says Katz, who got to work on a few of the action scenes, though they were primarily handled by her co-editor, Richard Learoyd. "You want to see the glint of the sword, you want to see who gets slashed and the movements of the bodies. It's like dance, and it has a rhythm of its own."

To bleed or not to bleed: Some of the film's violent content had to be toned down to appease the Chinese government, which had funded much of the China/ Hong Kong co-production. Indeed, **Fearless** ended up being released in a number of different versions in different territories.

Dreamgirls is different from other recent musicals in that it tells the story through song. Bill and I are both fans of the old musicals. Shots were held for a reasonable length of time and you could see people's bodies moving in the frame. If you're going to choreograph a number, you want to see the dance. And for a number like "Steppin' to the Bad Side," it was important not only to see the steps, but also to see the characters interacting with each other. You want to see the way Eddie Murphy and Anika Noni Rose are connecting with each other and starting a relationship. Bill and I wanted to be able to see all these things, to follow every step and capture the emotional expressions as well.

It worked the same way with "And I Am Telling You I'm Not Going." We had many takes and shot choices to choose from, but in the end, it was really about Jennifer Hudson. There's always a bit of finessing in the cutting room, but we mainly just stayed close on her because her performance was so powerful. Although she had never been in a movie, she was a singer, and she instinctively was able to give us the performance we were looking for. No matter what you're cutting, whether it's a musical or a drama, if you don't have the performances and good writing, you're not going to make it work. With **Dreamgirls**, although there was a huge amount of film, it all flowed because of how Bill chose to shoot the scenes. When it works in the camera, it'll work in the cutting room. I always know when they've had trouble on the set with the scene, because when I get it, I'm going to have trouble with it, too.

Each character took on a different tone in editing. When Eddie first comes on screen, he has a completely different vibe from the other characters. He is manic, and so his first →

DREAMGIRLS

Early on, Condon and Katz decided they wanted **Dreamgirls** to flow organically from one number to the next, allowing the songs to propel the narrative forward. Their visual approach underscored this idea, as Katz often opted not to cut at all. In the early moments of "Family," the camera swirls around Effie White (Jennifer Hudson) and her brother C.C. (Keith Robinson) in a lengthy, unbroken shot that allows the viewer to not only take in the performance, but also to see the actors' bodies move through space—an increasing rarity among contemporary screen musicals.

FEARLESS

While her co-editor Richard Learoyd handled most of the fight scenes in Ronny Yu's **Fearless**, Katz did get to try her hand at some of the action. While the cutting of these sequences was fairly rapid, Katz notes that there are certain essentials that must be shown in order to keep the audience's interest. "If somebody lifts a sword and slashes it, you want to see the sword, you want to see the glint, and you want to see the other person get slashed or dodge," she says. "It's like dance. It has a rhythm of its own."

KINSEY

Throughout **Kinsey**, we see the famous professor
and sex researcher (played by Liam Neeson)
teaching others how to apply his clinical, thoroughly
nonjudgmental interview techniques when gathering
people's sexual histories. Kinsey's methods are illustrated
in a series of rapid-fire montages, so tightly cut by Katz
that the viewer barely has enough time to register each
probing and provocative question delivered by Kinsey's
protégés (top to bottom: Peter Sarsgaard, Timothy
Hutton and Chris O'Donnell). Like **Gods and Monsters**
before it, **Kinsey** makes attention-grabbing use of black-
and-white interstitial footage in a way that adds a certain
meta-layer without distancing the viewer.

number is cut in a much more manic, energetic
way than, say, a scene of Beyoncé singing. When
Eddie's at the piano there's just such energy, and
I felt that energy had to be communicated in
the editing.

Because everybody is so familiar with the
music in **Dreamgirls** it was hard to take out a
section of music. We had to make it sound as
if we hadn't removed anything; it had to seem
effortless. There were a couple of instances
where we took out a piece of a song, and thanks
to our music editor, Paul Rabjohns, I don't think
you'd ever know. But it was trying at times. It's
hard to take out things that you love. But if the
movie feels 20 minutes too long (the first

cut of **Dreamgirls** was probably close to three
hours), you've got to cut those 20 minutes out.
There was a great scene of Eddie traveling,
which was intercut with his performance onstage.
It worked beautifully, but it felt too long. So
we lifted it. We hated doing that because the
scene was so good, but sometimes you have
to sacrifice a scene in order to make the movie
play better.

If **Dreamgirls** was like an operetta, then
Burlesque (2010) was more in the vein of a
standard musical built around a stage. It's faster,
shinier and bawdier, much more tuned in to the
way burlesque is itself. We applied a staccato
rhythm, because the numbers lent themselves

The breadth of Kinsey's research is illustrated by an intricately designed graphic sequence in which the camera sweeps across a map of the United States, as one interview subject after another spills his or her sexual secrets. "We spent a lot of time on that map," Katz recalls. "Every time you changed something, something else would change. It was a real challenge."

to that, as did the handheld camerawork. There were very few scenes in **Burlesque** in which the camera was not moving, which allowed us to quicken the pacing. It was a lot of fun yet very different from **Dreamgirls**, which had an entirely different rhythm.

Whether you're a director, an editor, or a cameraman, there's always a danger of getting pegged in this industry. I do **Dreamgirls** and everyone thinks I can only do musicals. I do **Candyman** and I get offered all the horror movies. What's great about Bill's career—and therefore mine, too—is that he does whatever interests him most, no matter what the genre. We've done horror, we've done drama, we've done musicals, and now, with **The Twilight Saga: Breaking Dawn**, we're working with visual effects. It's great to have the opportunity to work on so many different kinds of films. But no matter what the genre, I'm an editor, and it's my job to help create the best film I can. That's what I do, and I love doing it. ,,

Michael Kahn

"I can see the advantages, at least for these films, of working on the Avid. But I do think something's been lost with digital editing, I really do—the cogitation, the level of thought about how you should cut something."

While Michael Kahn is best known for his long-running collaboration with Steven Spielberg, the Brooklyn-born editor learned his craft on the set of the television sitcom **Hogan's Heroes** (1965–71). It was a fortuitous first gig; George C. Scott was such a fan of the series that he asked Kahn to edit his first feature, **Rage** (1972). Kahn has since won three Academy Awards for his work on **Raiders of the Lost Ark** (1981), **Schindler's List** (1993), and **Saving Private Ryan** (1998), and holds the record for most editing nominations overall (seven), having also been nominated for **Close Encounters of the Third Kind** (1977), **Empire of the Sun** (1987), **Fatal Attraction** (1987), and **Munich** (2005). Other credits amassed over the course of his four-decade career include **Eyes of Laura Mars** (1978, Irvin Kershner), **Poltergeist** (1982, Tobe Hooper), **The Goonies** (1985, Richard Donner), **Arachnophobia** (1990, Frank Marshall), **Twister** (1996, Jan de Bont), **The Spiderwick Chronicles** (2008, Mark Waters), and **Prince of Persia: The Sands of Time** (2010, Mike Newell).

Michael Kahn

" Honest to God, I knew nothing about editing when I started. I was almost fresh out of high school, and I was working at Desilu Productions, where a nice fellow by the name of Danny Kahn (no relation) told me, "In this town, if you want to survive, you've got to be in a union." So he put me in the editors' union, and I went to work assisting some editors, and I started learning the craft, since they'd pushed me into it.

Shortly afterward a personal friend of mine, Jerry London, caught a lucky break and cut the pilot of **Hogan's Heroes** (1965). And he said, "Mike, I don't want to be an editor. I want to be a director or a producer. If you assist me for the first six episodes, you'll be editor as of the seventh show." And that's exactly how it happened. On the seventh episode of **Hogan's Heroes**, I started editing. I was scared to death. I didn't know what I was doing. It's funny, you go in there and it's not as easy as you think it will be, going in.

I learned the craft and did about six years of **Hogan's Heroes**, and that's when I really learned how to edit. We had a producer who would tell me, "Never put in a cold cut." A cold cut isn't something you eat; it's when you cut to something where there's nothing happening. If you want to

overlap something, it should never be to a cold cut, because that stops the picture; it stops the forward movement. And he also said, "Never overlap a joke." If you have a line, let the line finish, and then go to the reaction. And that's not a cold cut, because you're going there for a laugh. We had a lot of rules like that, and they stood me in good stead.

The most valuable lesson I've learned is to not be afraid of the film. Sometimes you get reams of film and it's all over the place. I had to learn how to focus solely on the takes for a particular scene—whether it's four, five or 20—and just deal with those. I learned to compartmentalize the film in my mind, and that made me much more secure with the film itself. I focus on the footage in front of me, without worrying about the other parts of the film. Occasionally I'll put in echoes, meaning I'll plant something in reel one and echo it in reel eight. It's a device that structures the film and helps the viewer recall what's happened before. But otherwise, there's nothing but that scene in front of me. You can only do one cut at a time.

For a long time, psychologically, I never felt I was good enough. All the other editors I worked

HOGAN'S HEROES
Kahn's first editing job was on the TV sitcom **Hogan's Heroes**, which he worked on for six years, during which he learned the importance of not using a cold cut (a cut to a shot with nothing happening) and of not cutting too quickly from a joke to a reaction. It proved to be an excellent training ground for editing features, not least because George C. Scott, a **Hogan's Heroes** fan, wound up asking Kahn to cut his film **Rage.**

with were so sure of themselves; they were all so well spoken and loquacious. I could never talk like that. I never felt that I was as good as they were. That feeling stayed with me for a long time. Even today, I work very hard to be the best I can be, because I'm not sure somebody else can't do it better. The only time I knew I was OK was after I worked for Steven Spielberg on a couple of films. I thought, this is a really sharp guy, sharp as a tack, so if he accepted me, I felt that I must have had something to contribute. And that's when I started feeling good about myself.

I can't explain how I do what I do. I suppose there's some circuitry in my brain that allows me to appreciate when things are harmonious, when the rhythm is smooth, when I'm telling the story with the visuals. Something tells you when it's right. I wasn't schooled for that; it's just something that's in me. I'll just get a feeling that the way I cut it this time is good enough that I can show it to Steven. You've got to satisfy yourself before you can show it to the boss. It's got to be OK for you.

I often tell Steven, "Let me make mistakes. Let me not be afraid to try something different or innovative, because if I'm just being conventional, then I'm not helping you." So he lets me do that. He tells me what he'd like, of course, and if I feel that I want to try something else, that's OK. He can throw it out, which he sometimes does, but then again, he may accept it. At the very least, he has something to work against.

Steven always tells people, "I shoot for the editing room." That's his phrase. He shoots enough film so that we can go any way we want to in the editing room. People often forget that a movie is not a movie until it's edited. They think that if you shoot it, it's a movie. But it's not. It's got to be put together. You have to think about where you want the scenes to fall and the reactions to appear. There's an incredible amount to do in order to get the best possible effect.

The first time I worked with him was on **Close Encounters of the Third Kind** (1977). There's a moment in the film where Neary (Richard Dreyfuss) is running up the hill, trying to get to the other side where the spaceships are going to land. →

A brief history of the Moviola

Tool of the trade: The Moviola was originally conceived in 1917 by inventor Iwan Serrurier as a home-movie projector, though its hefty price tag—due in part to the wooden cabinet it came in—made it an impractical purchase for most of the general public. In 1924, Serrurier retooled the device as an editing machine, the first of which was sold to Douglas Fairbanks Studios for $125 (about $4,500 today).

One frame at a time: The device's chief innovation was that it allowed editors to view their film, frame by individual film, as they were editing. This did not become a crucial selling point until the advent of sound in 1928, which made precision cutting of paramount importance. The Moviola was quickly adopted by studios and remained the industry standard until the rise of electronic editing systems in the 1970s.

News on the march: Moviola sales spiked during World War II, as newsreels, military and propaganda films boosted demand for portable moviemaking equipment in the trenches. Before and after this period, Serrurier continued to add enhancements to his product, such as sound heads, rewinders, synchronizers and viewers for different shooting formats.

Pro and Kahn: Though he recently began using the Avid, Kahn has been perhaps the Moviola's greatest champion among editors, sticking with the device long after his colleagues moved on to digital platforms. As George Lucas told *Time*'s Richard Corliss in a 2006 interview, "Michael Kahn can cut faster on a Moviola than anybody can cut on an Avid."

For the life of me, I couldn't put together that sequence. I don't know what it was, but I couldn't get it together. So I went to Steven and said, "I'm not sure how to do this," and he said, "How refreshing it is to have an editor who says he's not sure what to do." He appreciated that I wasn't ashamed to show vulnerability by asking for help.

We've been working together for 34 years now. I'm very comfortable with him, and he's comfortable with me. It's loose all the time with Steven. He's open and he's loose. If I do disagree with him or another director, I know to do it in a circuitous way. You've got to use careful verbiage, such as, "Do you think this is OK? Do you think we're doing the right thing?" Frontal assaults aren't good. I don't think anybody likes it, though a lot of editors do it.

I'll never forget the response to **Schindler's List** (1993) when we screened it at the Academy. The film ended and there was just silence. I've never been to a film where there was just silence. I heard some whimpers here and there, but people were just so taken by the film. It's good to affect an audience. That's the real joy of film

editing—you're in there, editing with your director, but you're really doing it for the audience. The audience is what matters.

There was one particular scene that we decided to cut out. Oskar Schindler is on the phone in his factory, and he hears there's a train coming down the track, carrying Jews evacuated from a concentration camp. And they all run down to meet the train, and they open the railcar, and inside are all these Jews frozen to death. My God, that scene was so heavy. I was playing music underneath, a Hebraic song, and it just broke you up; it was too much. Steven decided to keep that scene out, and I agreed with him. There's only so much you can make an audience endure. You don't want to hit people over the head with drama or overdo it; then it becomes melodramatic.

We shot the opening sequence of **Saving Private Ryan** (1998) in Ireland. Steven and the cinematographer, Janusz Kaminski, used different styles of film on each take. There would be a 24-frame take, and then they'd shoot some at 12 frames, and then they'd try it with a 45-degree shutter. There were four to five different

> **"...I do think something's been lost with digital editing, I really do—the cogitation, the level of thought about how you should cut something."**

techniques involved, and what I was able to do was to intermix all these different styles, and boy, what a thrill it was. I couldn't start the scene until I had the 12 frames optically brought up to 24 frames, the regular speed, so when that footage came in, it looked like it had been shot using old World War II shutters. It looked so real. And when the soldiers went underwater, we used the underwater footage, and then I put bubbles in.

After I cut the opening, we went to an air base outside London to shoot the rest of the picture. Every morning, Steven would come in and watch that scene. He wouldn't make any changes; he'd just watch the scene. We weren't clear why he kept watching it. I mean, was there something I should have done better? And finally I asked, "Steven, why are you looking at that scene?" And he said, "Well, it's a great scene, but I don't want to duplicate it later in the film. I want to do something different." You never know what's on the mind of a director.

I've always edited on film—until now. We've just made a change. On **War Horse** (2011) and **The Adventures of Tintin: The Secret of the**

Unicorn (2011), we're doing it on the Avid. Steven's a traditionalist. He loves the feel of film, the smell of it. There's something about film that takes you back to the beginning. I've done so many pictures on film, it's like that song, "Because it's second nature to me now." We still have a million feet of film sitting here in case we have to go back to film.

I can see the advantages, at least for these films, of working on the Avid. But I do think something's been lost with digital editing, I really do—the cogitation, the level of thought about how you should cut something. You have to study the material more on film, because you don't want to make that cut unless you're sure. I thought a lot more when I was using a Moviola. On the Avid, if you don't like it, you just press Apple-Z and you try it again, as often as you like. And I'm not sure that's good for an editor, because he's not given the opportunity to really formulate, in his own thoughts, how he'd like to present it to the director. Instead, he does a lot of versions, and the director makes up his mind. It's like that old joke about the Chinese →

SCHINDLER'S LIST
Editing **Schindler's List** proved an emotional experience for both Kahn and Spielberg, to the point where they at times found it difficult to run through scenes together in the cutting room. Their method was to present the film's reconstruction of the Holocaust without pushing its horrors or the drama too hard. At one point, Spielberg opted to remove a particularly grueling scene Kahn had cut together, in which Schindler discovers a train full of Jews who have frozen to death. "My God, that scene was so heavy," Kahn recalls. "Steven decided to keep that scene out, and I agreed with him. There's only so much you can make an audience endure."

SAVING PRIVATE RYAN

The Normandy landing sequence that opens **Saving Private Ryan** was shot using a number of different techniques (including shooting at 12 frames per second with a 45-degree shutter) designed to give the film the look of old World War II footage. Kahn describes the memory of assembling the scene, and blending the unique camera formats, with almost childlike enthusiasm. "There's a shot of a guy who gets shot in the helmet. He takes his helmet off, looks at it, then puts it back on his head, and then he gets shot in the head through the helmet. That was incredible. That kind of thing from Steven is really, really good," Kahn says. "Any editor in town would give his left arm to cut that can of footage."

"Steven's a traditionalist. He loves the feel of film, the smell of it. There's something about film that takes you back to the beginning."

restaurant—use this from Column A, or use this from Column B. It's funny, but it's true.

I don't mean to demean anybody by saying this, but I think the editor has more to say on film than on the Avid. The editor has less responsibility now. The director can come into the room and sit with the editor and say what he'd like, and the editor stops thinking about what *he* would like. What you don't want in an editor is a visual typist, someone who's just typing out the images, but that's what the editor's become. Look, I understand everything is going digital; there's no way out of it. But I think my film background was very good for me. You take a kid who comes into the editing room and you try to talk to them about

film, and they don't know what you're talking about. Ninety percent of them don't know film. They don't know the history of the business.

The first time I was nominated for an Oscar was for **Close Encounters of the Third Kind**. I was sitting there, praying I wouldn't win, because the thought of getting up in front of all those people just scared the hell out of me. Luckily, someone else won. But it's very exciting, because you're not in a room anymore; you're sitting there with thousands of people and millions watching on television, and you're part of the industry. Before that moment, you're not part of the industry. You're sitting in a room, in my case a dark room, but you're not part of the industry;

you're just part of that one film. But when you get honored, you feel 10 feet tall. And you say, "gee, I got an Oscar, isn't that great?" And then you wonder if you'll ever get another one, and you never think you will. I was one of the lucky ones. I work for a director who makes great films, and who's made enough films that I've had chances to win awards. You don't work to win an Oscar, obviously; you work to come out with a good picture. But thanks to Steven, I have a whole career. Without him, I'd still be a good editor, but I wouldn't be working on the kind of material he gives me. ""

CLOSE ENCOUNTERS OF THE THIRD KIND

This was the first film Kahn cut for Spielberg. Kahn found himself having trouble cutting together the scene of Neary and friends running up the hill to the spaceship landing zone. When he admitted as much to the director, Spielberg responded, "How refreshing it is to have an editor who says he's not sure what to do," before explaining what he wanted to see in the sequence. Thus began a collaboration that has lasted 34 years.

Joel Cox

"Today, every up-and-comer wants to edit right away. But experience is important, and you have to do many films before you can become comfortable and really, truly understand the art of editing."

Joel Cox received his first screen credit at the age of six weeks, when he appeared in Mervyn LeRoy's **Random Harvest** (1942). He began his career in film production in 1961 in the mailroom at Warner Bros. and eventually worked his way into the studio's editorial department, serving as assistant editor on films such as Sam Peckinpah's **The Wild Bunch** (1969), and Francis Ford Coppola's **The Rain People** (1969).

Cox received his first feature-editing credit on Dick Richards' **Farewell, My Lovely** (1975), co-edited with Walter Thompson. But it was an assistant-editing position on **The Outlaw Josey Wales** (1976) that introduced him to Clint Eastwood, initiating a collaboration that includes the recent biographical drama **J. Edgar** (2012), edited with Gary Roach, also Cox's collaborator on **Letters from Iwo Jima** (2006), **Changeling** (2008), **Gran Torino** (2008), and **Invictus** (2009). Cox won the Academy Award for Best Editing for Eastwood's **Unforgiven** (1992) and was nominated for **Million Dollar Baby** (2004), and he has also cut the director's **Pale Rider** (1985), **Bird** (1988), **A Perfect World** (1993), **The Bridges of Madison County** (1995), **Mystic River** (2003), and **Flags of Our Fathers** (2006). His other credits include Buddy Van Horn's **Pink Cadillac** (1989) and James Keach's **The Stars Fell on Henrietta** (1995).

Joel Cox

" A lot of people won't agree with me, but my one belief about the Academy Awards is that whatever wins Best Picture should also win Best Director and Best Editing. When all is said and done, and the shooting is finished, the editor and the director sit in the room and create the final film. It doesn't make editing any more important than acting or writing. But I believe editing represents the last write on the script, and a lot of writers would agree with me on that point. Of course, we as editors can't do anything without the two or three hundred other people on the crew. We just happen to have the job that's at the end of the funnel.

The director–editor relationship is a very special one. The director, of course, has relationships with everyone on the crew, but it's not as constant or sustained as it is with the editor, when the two spend day after day working together in the cutting room. The relationship doesn't always work out. I've seen a lot of editors taken off films throughout my career, and most of the time, it wasn't because the editor wasn't a good editor; it was because the relationship didn't work. I've been very fortunate, working with Clint Eastwood for the past 35 years.

Clint likes the editing to be fluid, so that a story just comes together. You'll see a lot of editing today with quick cuts and jump cuts, and the editor will suddenly go in for a closeup. It's what we call "cutting for the best line reading," and Clint always says that sometimes, the best line reading doesn't need to be in there. Maybe you're putting a sequence together and you need to stay in a particular shot, and it may not contain the best line reading. But the director, the actor, and the editor are the only ones who know there's a better one. If you simply went by the best line reading, you could go from a closeup to a wide shot to a medium shot, and the fluidity of the sequence would fall apart. And fluidity is very important. If the audience sees a particularly jarring shot, it takes them out of the story. So Clint and I are always trying to be smooth, so that it just flows like molasses. You know what a great cut is? A cut you didn't see. You didn't see it because you're so engrossed in the story, you don't even realize we're editing. To me, that's what great editing is.

Clint is an actor first, and he believes that when an actor runs through a scene over and over again, the performance starts to fall apart. That's why he doesn't do a lot of takes when he's directing. You're liable to capture something in the first few takes that you can't repeat one hundred takes down the road. But for an actor, Clint also has no vanity: If he's directing himself in a picture, he will absolutely cut himself out of a scene if he feels it moves the story along. Prominent actors sometimes become powerful enough that they insist on having lots of closeups. Clint always says, "Man, we've got a 40-foot screen. We don't need to play a film in closeup." He prefers to let the film breathe, take the audience on a ride, and let them enjoy the story.

Clint and I both agree that digital editing is perhaps the greatest thing that's happened to film. In the old days, when you cut on film, if you wanted to undo a change, you'd never get it back exactly to where you had it. Here, we save everything. I taught Gary Roach never to throw anything away. Save everything. It just saves it in the bin, and it doesn't take up any space; it's just numbers. But it may save you in the end.

Gary and I did something on **J. Edgar** that we've never done before, which is split a scene in two. It was a long scene, and I took the first half and he took the second, because we had nothing else to do and it didn't make sense for one of us to sit and do nothing. And when we joined the two halves, they went together like butter—no one could say where my work ended and his began. And that's because he learned my style, as my assistant. Sometimes, I can look at a film and I can see where two different editors have cut it, because everyone has a different sense of rhythm and structure. I'm fortunate because Gary's learned from me, though of course he still brings his own ideas to the table, which is great, because I don't want him to mask me. I want him to be his own person.

I myself came up through this industry working as an assistant for a long time with →

Learning the ropes

A child of the Hollywood studio system, Cox counts not only Ralph Winters (see Legacy, page 118) but also the following editors among his esteemed mentors. Sam O'Steen enjoyed a lengthy collaboration with Mike Nichols, editing 12 of the director's films including **The Graduate** (1967), **Catch-22** (1970), **Carnal Knowledge** (1971), **Working Girl** (1988) and **Regarding Henry** (1991). He received three Oscar nominations for editing Nichols' **Who's Afraid of Virginia Woolf?** (1966) and **Silkwood** (1983), and Roman Polanski's **Chinatown** (1974).

Walter Thompson received Oscar nominations for editing **This Above All** (1942) and **The Nun's Story** (1959) and edited more than 60 films and TV programs over his 45-year career, including **Tin Pan Alley** (1940), **Jane Eyre** (1943), **The Wonderful World of the Brothers Grimm** (1962), **Fat City** (1972) and **The Paper Chase** (1973). His final credit, **Farewell, My Lovely** (1975), was Cox's first.

Ferris Webster was a frequent collaborator with such filmmakers as Vincente Minnelli, John Frankenheimer, John Sturges and Clint Eastwood in a career that spanned more than seventy titles. He received three Oscar nominations for editing **Blackboard Jungle** (1955), **The Manchurian Candidate** (1962) and **The Great Escape** (1963).

William H. Ziegler edited nearly a hundred films including Alfred Hitchcock's **Rope** (1948) and **Starngers on a Train** (1951), Nicholas Ray's **Rebel Without a Cause** (1955), and several musicals—two of which, **The Music Man** (1962) and **My Fair Lady** (1964), earned him Oscar nominations. He was also nominated for **Auntie Mame** (1958).

BIRD

This film was an unusually complex film for Joel Cox to edit not only because of its time-shuffling structure, but because Clint Eastwood wanted to preserve the integrity of the jazz music performed in the film and not merely cut it into pieces to serve the story. More often than not, the story ended up serving the music, as Cox (working closely with music editor Don Harris and composer Lennie Niehaus) would recut the picture to suit any track trims or adjustments.

a number of really good editors, like Bill Ziegler, Sam O'Steen, and Ralph Winters. I watched Bill cut **The Music Man** (1962) and I watched Sam cut **Who's Afraid of Virginia Woolf?** (1966). Sam showed how he physically cut the film, how he ran the footage through his Moviola, made the cuts and ran it through the synchronizer. He taught me my style of editing. Today, every up-and-comer wants to edit right away. But experience is important, and you have to do many films before you can become comfortable and really, truly understand the art of editing. Anybody can put two different pieces of film together—if you sat down here with no editing experience, within a few hours, I could get you to make an edit. Would it be the correct edit for the scene? Maybe, maybe not. Until you do it, you'll never know. But it can't be just a guessing game. It takes years of experience, and the sad thing I see now is that some editors lack the patience

to truly learn the art of it. They just slam it all together so that it becomes a trial-and-error exercise, and that's not really editing.

Are our films fashionable with young people today? No. We know our audience is 30-up. We're not hiding anything. Younger audiences who have grown up on MTV and video games, they don't want to see a story unfold. They couldn't sit through **The Bridges of Madison County**, or **A Perfect World**, or **Changeling**. They always say it's slow. Well, no, it's not slow. It's a real story about real people's lives. You can't do the kinds of films Clint and I are doing in an MTV style, because you would lose all the emotion. I sometimes kiddingly call Clint and myself the "masters of emotion," because all the films we've done are emotional films—this next one, **J. Edgar**, is full of it—and emotion isn't cut the same way that action is. An emotional film is much harder to edit than an action film; it's all

about timing and individual moments, when to
cut and when not to cut. Walter Thompson, with
whom I co-edited **Farewell, My Lovely** (1975),
and Ferris Webster, whom I assisted on **The
Outlaw Josey Wales** (1976)—those two guys
showed me all about editing for emotion.

I wound up doing all the recuts with Clint on
The Outlaw Josey Wales, and that was when our
relationship came together. He was impressed
because I did all the splicing myself, and
because of my music background, from working
with Kenny Wilhoit on **The F.B.I.** (1965), I knew
how to track the film, to actually take music and
make it fit the picture, which is different than
just taking a fresh score and dropping it in. I
had been fortunate enough to grow up in an
old-school studio and do almost every job on the
Warner Bros. lot. I started in the mailroom, and I
also worked in sound effects, ADR, and music. By
the time I got to the cutting room I think I had a

leg up on some of the other editors, because
I had a more complete understanding of what
editing is.

My music background served me very well
on **Bird** (1988). Clint brought Charlie Parker's
music over here from Paris in a very raw state,
and I knew that cutting the music correctly was
going to be a massive job. Some of those songs
were five or six minutes long, and there were 15
or 20 of them, and we needed to cut them down.
Now, you can't just cut into a jazz song anywhere;
it's not like cutting into a pop song and taking out
a set of lyrics. You have to take out just the right
bars so it maintains the proper structure. So I
would tell our composer, Lennie Niehaus, "OK,
here's a song that's six minutes long and it needs
to be three." Lennie would listen to it and tell me,
"I can only get this much out of it," and I'd say,
"Fine, I'll take it," and then I would recut the
picture to match. It was all done with the →

> "Are our films fashionable with young people today? No. We know our audience is 30-up. We're not hiding anything."

purpose of keeping the integrity of the music intact. The first cut of **Bird** ran to three hours and 17 minutes, and we brought it down to two hours 42 minutes, which is where it stayed. Clint said, "I know it's a small-audience film, but I also know that at a certain point, I'm going to have to cut either the story or the music, and I don't want to do either." So we went out at two 42.

Clint gives Gary and me very little instruction when we're doing a first edit, because he knows we can always make changes easily enough afterward. He tells us, "I want to see what you see, because you may see something I don't." When you've done enough of Clint's films, you get pretty used to his style, but there are still times when I'll wonder exactly what he was thinking on a particular scene, and that's the creative part of him at work. But he comes in as prepared as any director. Clint gets everything. He knows in his mind exactly what he wants. People often say, "Well, he's camera-cutting." No, he doesn't camera-cut. He shoots all the angles all the way through.

When Clint was doing his research on **Flags of Our Fathers** (2006), he kept reading about Gen.

Kuribayashi, which became the genesis of **Letters from Iwo Jima** (2006). So while we were in post on **Flags**, waiting for all the effects to be finished, we went off and shot this other film. Because the two films were made concurrently, there were times when he shot extra footage on one film that he knew was going to appear in the other film. We thought it would be very bold to shoot both sides of the war in such a way that the films wouldn't detract from each other, but that they would create the structure together.

Letters from Iwo Jima was challenging because it was entirely in Japanese. It was the first film I co-edited with Gary, and Clint said to both of us, "Look, you'll get the rhythm of the dialogue. Just listen to it." So we did, and he was right, because if you listened to it, you could understand what was being communicated in each shot. When we were finished, they brought in an interpreter, and we ended up having to fix only four words. It was tough work, though, as were the French sequences on **Hereafter** (2010).

Clint gives me the material and allows me to try different things when putting it together— such as in **Mystic River**, when I decided to fade

**FLAGS OF OUR FATHERS;
LETTERS FROM IWO JIMA**
These two films were not only produced concurrently, but designed to complement each other as halves of a diptych. Footage from one film was often incorporated into the other, and Cox's editing choices deliberately reinforced the notion that neither film by itself—which is to say, neither an American perspective nor a Japanese perspective—would present a complete picture of one of the defining conflicts of World War II. In **Flags of Our Fathers** (opposite), the raising of the flag on Mt. Suribachi is presented and deconstructed in close-up; in **Letters from Iwo Jima** (right), the same event is shown as a tiny, insignificant speck in the distance.

to white after the scene in which Sean Penn learns that his daughter is dead. It may not always work, but sometimes it does. Another example: As originally written, **Hereafter** was supposed to end with the mother and the boy. But when I cut it together, it didn't entirely work for me. So I cut it a different way, so that it ended with Matt Damon and Cécile De France, and I showed Clint and told him, "This is the way I think this film should end. It's about them, and it's a love story." And he said I was right, and that was how the film ended. You see, Clint allows the creative part to be creative. Sometimes he'll go back to the way he wanted something originally, but he doesn't want to just take editorial and squelch it. I remember cutting a scene together on **Unforgiven** (1992), and he said, "Wow, I didn't really see this scene that way, but I like it. Don't touch that."

By contrast, there are some directors who are so hands-on that in dailies, they'll tell you, "I want this and this and this." I remember when I was working with Dick Richards on **Rafferty and the Gold Dust Twins** (1975) and **Farewell, My Lovely**, he used to tell me, "I want three frames of this and four frames of that." So one time, to show him exactly what that literally meant, I compiled a bunch of footage, from camera blowouts and such, and I structured about five feet of it at the end of the last reel of dailies. And when he saw it, he said, "What was that?" And I said, "Well, that was your three frames of this and four frames of that." And we laughed, because we had a great relationship and he got a big kick out of it.

I've been very fortunate—just look at the people I've worked for. Look at the films I've worked on. I didn't earn it; it's not whether I was good or not. I think part of the job is being in the right place at the right time. A lot of editors would say, "Boy I'd really like to have that job." But you can't sit on your laurels. You've got to work. I'm here because I continue to do so.

HEREAFTER

Editors rarely interfere with a script built on intricate, interlocking storylines. Still, it was Cox who suggested a deviation from Peter Morgan's screenplay for **Hereafter**, which he felt would be more effective if it ended with the scene in which George (Matt Damon) and Marie (Cécile De France) meet for the first time. "I said, 'When you see this, this film ends right here,'" Cox says. "It's about them. The love story."

UNFORGIVEN

One of the most challenging scenes to edit in **Unforgiven** was the confrontation between Little Bill (Gene Hackman) and English Bob (Richard Harris), in which the sheriff forces the gunman to surrender his firearm and then brutally beats and kicks him in the streets. Eastwood and his crew produced 13,000 feet of film for the scene alone, presenting Cox with the challenge of maintaining tension, cutting the action together and capturing the reactions of onlookers. "You're fortunate if you've got that much material to work with, but it's a very time-consuming thing," Cox says.

Ralph E. Winters

The editor of nearly 80 films over the course of his 70-year career, Ralph E. Winters evinced a deft, professional touch with a wide range of genres, encompassing spectacular period epics such as **Ben-Hur** (1959), classic musicals such as **Seven Brides for Seven Brothers** (1954), and sophisticated slapstick comedies such as **The Pink Panther** (1963).

Born in Toronto in 1909, he was barely 20 when he went to work at MGM, where his father had a job as a tailor. He began his editing career in 1941 with Harold S. Bucquet's **The Penalty**, which was followed by a string of B pictures including Fred Zinnemann's directing debut, the 1942 crime drama **Kid Glove Killer**, and Jules Dassin's romantic comedy **The Affairs of Martha** (1942). His breakthrough credit, however, came in 1944 with **Gaslight**, George Cukor's memorable psychological thriller with Charles Boyer and Ingrid Bergman.

Winters went on to cut a string of films for Roy Rowland, including **Our Vines Have Tender Grapes** (1945), **Boys' Ranch** (1946), **The Romance of Rosy Ridge** (1947), **Killer McCoy** (1947) and **Tenth Avenue Angel** (1948). He also edited Mervyn LeRoy's **Little Women** (1949) and Stanley Donen and Gene Kelly's classic New York-set musical **On the Town** (1949).

He won the Academy Award for best editing on his first try with Compton Bennett and Andrew Marton's adaptation of **King Solomon's Mines** (1950). The next decade of his career were marked by such high-profile films as the Cole Porter musicals **Kiss Me Kate** (1953) and **High Society** (1956); Donen's **Seven Brides for Seven Brothers**; and the Roman epics **Quo Vadis** (LeRoy, 1951) and **Ben-Hur** (William Wyler). The last film (co-edited with John D. Dunning) represents some of Winters' most impressive work, not least for its legendary chariot-race sequence, and won him a second editing Oscar.

01 Ben Hur

02 Ben Hur

Executive Suite (1954), Jailhouse Rock (1957), and Butterfield 8 (1960) were among Winters' other notable credits during this period. In 1963, he began editing films for the writer-director Blake Edwards, starting with The Pink Panther and its 1964 sequel, A Shot in the Dark; their long-running collaboration, by no means limited to comedy, also included The Great Race (1965), What Did You Do in the War, Daddy? (1966), The Party (1968), 10 (1979), S.O.B.. (1981), Victor Victoria (1982), and Curse of the Pink Panther (1983).

The ever-prolific editor continued to work with other filmmakers as well, cutting The Thomas Crown Affair (1968), Norman Jewison's romantic caper starring Steve McQueen and Faye Dunaway; Jack Lemmon's Kotch (1971), with Walter Matthau; Billy Wilder's version of the oft-adapted The Front Page (1974), featuring Lemmon and Matthau; and John Guillerman's 1976 remake of King Kong.

Winters was a founder of the American Cinema Editors in 1951 and received the guild's career achievement in 1991, four years before he edited his final feature, Cutthroat Island. In 2001, he published his memoir, *Some Cutting Remarks: Seventy Years a Film Editor*. Winters died in 2004.

03 Seven Brides for Seven Brothers

04 The Thomas Crowne Affair

William Chang Suk-ping

"I used a lot of slow-motion in **Chungking Express**. It can create a very emotional effect, just as dissolves can as well. I always try to use these techniques to deepen emotion, rather than merely using technique for technique's sake."

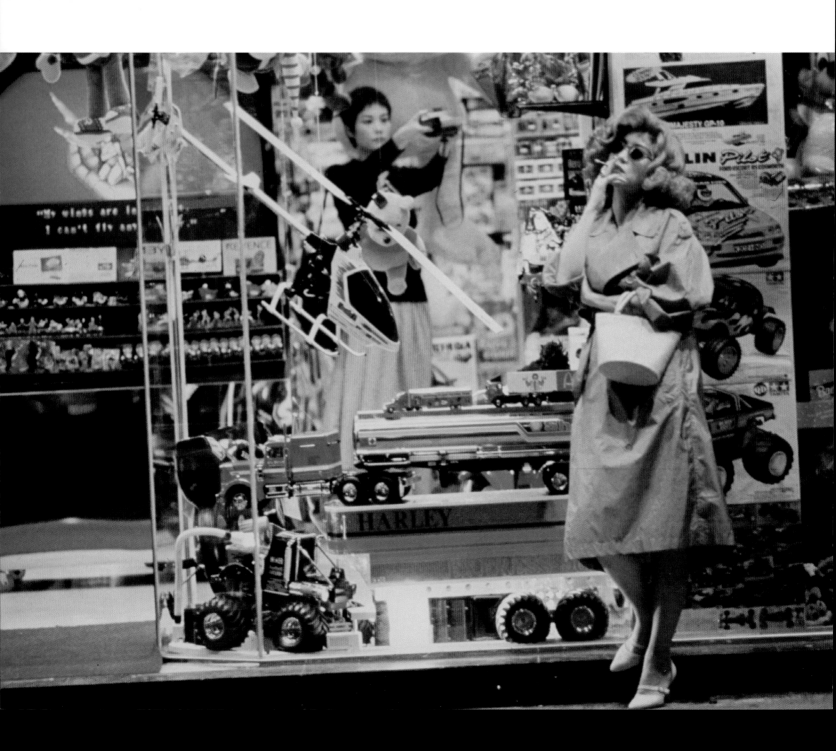

Born in 1953 in Hong Kong, William Chang Suk-ping knew from the age of 14 that he wanted to be in the film business. After studying film at the Vancouver School of Art (now the Emily Carr University of Art and Design), he returned to Hong Kong, where he has established himself as one of the few below-the-line craftsmen who works as both a production designer and a film editor, often on the same project. He received his first feature-editing credit on Wong Kar-wai's **As Tears Go By** (1988), launching a collaboration that continues to this day: Chang has also handled dual roles on Wong's **Chungking Express** (1994), **Fallen Angels** (1995), **Happy Together** (1997), **In the Mood for Love** (2000), **2046** (2004) and **My Blueberry Nights** (2007). He has also edited Stanley Kwan's **Lan Yu** (2001) and **Everlasting Regret** (2005); Zhou Sun's **Zhou Yu's Train** (2002); and Lee Daniels' **Shadowboxer** (2005). His most recent credit is Wong's upcoming biographical martial-arts drama **The Grandmasters** (2012).

William Chang Suk-ping

" Two directors I greatly admire are Pier Paolo Pasolini and Satyajit Ray. Pasolini's editing is very loose, raw, and even objective at times. There are many long takes and long conversations, and it's very fragmented; the continuation from scene to scene is not obvious. It's in pieces, but somehow it works. And I love Ray's lyricism. He's very sensitive to small details of human feeling and behavior, which is something I've tried to be as well. These influences are somehow always in the back of my mind when I'm editing a scene, and they start to emerge subconsciously. It's very difficult to analyze how this happens. Sometimes a scene ends up looking too similar to something I've seen in a past film, and I'll try to alter it or give it a different look by adding a dissolve or a freeze-frame.

I very seldom watch American films. There are a lot of them in Hong Kong, but I try not to watch them, and I try to avoid editing in a mainstream or commercial style. The fun of editing, for me, is being able to do something different. Editing is just fun. I don't take it too seriously. I love that nobody can tell me what to do. I can do anything and experiment with different types of cutting. Rhythm, for me, is a matter of instinct. There are

no formulas. When I start editing a film, I might play around for two weeks before suddenly an idea strikes me and I follow it, and that's when the real editing begins.

I never want to open a scene in a conventional way. Even if Wong Kar-wai shoots a traditional establishing shot, my tendency is to take it out. I try to find an alternative, unless there are not enough shots to begin with. But once I take out the establishing shot, somehow, the basic cutting of a scene, such as a conversation, can be very interesting. I'm not moving around a lot; I'm just listening to the conversation and looking at how the actors react. But even then, I might add something to make it a bit less conventional, such as cutting away mid-conversation to an empty shot, or adding unrelated dialogue, or varying the lengths of shots so that they're not symmetrical.

Wong and I were friends for about six or seven years before he became a director, so we knew each other very well by the time he got started. Every day after work, he would call me, and we would go out and eat and drink until morning, always talking about films. So we came to know what we liked and didn't like about cinema, and how we wanted our films to be. At that time Wong was a scriptwriter and I was a production

CHUNGKING EXPRESS

Wong Kar-wai and his then-regular director of photography, Christopher Doyle, filmed **Chungking Express** during a two-month break during post-production on his martial-arts epic **Ashes of Time** (1994). The improvised, free-form staging of the scene in which Faye Wong cleans Tony Leung's apartment proved typical of the "very random and free" method in which Wong Kar-wai shot the movie, and Chang followed suit in the cutting room, using frequent jump cuts and assembling scenes in an instinctual, if sometimes counterintuitive fashion. Because Chang never plays music when editing, Faye Wong's cover of The Cranberries' "Dreams" was laid over the scene after it was cut.

designer; I didn't know he was going to be a director, or that I was going to be an editor.

As Tears Go By (1988) was Wong's first film and the first film I edited. I was the production designer, and he had a deadline to meet and no time to edit, so he asked me to cut it. So for both of us, it was an experiment. On the set, he used different kinds of angles and lenses, and I tried to envision ways that he could be more experimental, freer to do what he wanted. I brought that thinking into the cutting room, too. Because it was my first editing job, I was very ambitious and tried to incorporate a lot of things, just to show people how much I knew. It was a very self-indulgent process.

Production design is a way of giving a particular look to the film, and editing is just a different way of doing the same thing, using rhythm and timing, and structure. The two never come into conflict. Doing both actually makes a lot of sense—when I'm doing the production design, I control the colors, and when I'm editing, I control the color grading. I wind up being able to give an entire look to the film. And because I'm on the set every day, I know exactly what he's shot.

It was very exciting to work on **Chungking Express** (1994), which Wong shot over a few weeks during a break from **Ashes of Time**.

I hadn't edited a film for him since **As Tears Go By**, but I told him I wanted to cut this one because it interested me and would give me a lot of room to experiment. The way he shot it was very random and free. What Faye Wong did in that apartment-cleaning scene, for instance, was completely unstaged. I was there every day during shooting, and my impression was that I should cut it in a similarly random fashion, and so I ended up using a lot of jump cuts.

When Wong shoots a scene a certain way, I sometimes feel a bit rebellious. I try not to cut the scene the way he shot it. I try to do something else, something better than the way he shot it. It's very childish of me, but Wong's okay with it. He's very broad-minded, and he gives me a very free hand in editing. Still, I was surprised on **Chungking Express**, when he accepted almost everything I gave him without asking any questions.

In general, Wong never wants to look at a scene until I've cut the whole thing. I like it that way—I don't want the director sitting behind me while I'm working. After I've done the first round, we'll talk about it. Sometimes he'll change it a little bit, and sometimes he won't change it at all. I used a lot of slow motion in **Chungking** →

Jet Tone Production

> "Instead of music, I always have this Chinese poetry in my head, and it gives me a rhythm, a feeling, a mood that I can cut to."

Express. It can create a very emotional effect, just as dissolves can as well. I always try to use these techniques to deepen emotion, rather than merely using technique for technique's sake. For instance, in one scene from **In the Mood for Love** (2000), Maggie Cheung finishes talking to Tony Leung and leaves the apartment. I used three very short, fast dissolves to convey a sense of her departure. For me, these dissolves feel very regretful—you talk, time goes by, and then you leave. It's as if you did nothing, as if you didn't talk in the first place.

I'm not really a music person. I don't listen to music or understand it. I can remember music from films, but I can't remember any other kind of music, if there are no visuals to accompany it. But when I'm editing, the visuals sing to me. I always cut the scenes first and then add the music in later. If the scene is cut well, the music will match it perfectly.

Instead of music, I always have this Chinese poetry in my head, and it gives me a rhythm, a feeling, a mood that I can cut to. I always follow these poetic rhythms when I'm trying to figure out, for example, whether a shot should be longer or shorter. In Tang Shi poetry, one sentence can mean something, but the foreign translation of that sentence could mean something entirely different; this is mirrored for me in editing by the way in which two totally different scenes can echo each other or be put together.

I cut every film on a Steenbeck up through **Happy Together** (1997), and then I switched to digital editing on **In the Mood for Love**. I found that digital editing allowed me to try a lot of different things in a very short amount of time. I have no patience; I want to see results immediately. On a Steenbeck, it would take me three months to edit a film. On digital it's faster, perhaps only one-and-a-half to two months, depending on how much footage there is. And Wong shoots a lot of footage, so digital editing is much more efficient. I remember cutting on film being very painful and tedious. You'd wind up crawling on the floor just to find a single frame.

I don't know why I decided to cut **In the Mood for Love** the way I did. For some reason, I felt it should be very, very subtle, and provide the viewer with less information than usual. The Tang Shi poetry especially came out during →

CHUNGKING EXPRESS
Chang Suk-ping deployed a number of blurred-motion effects on Wong Kar-wai's **Chungking Express**, as in this shot of a cop (Takeshi Kaneshiro) chasing a suspect through the bustling streets of Hong Kong. "Slow motion is normally used to smooth a transition from one place to the other," Chang says. "But for me, it can create a very emotional effect. I always try to use these techniques to deepen emotion, rather than merely using technique for technique's sake."

MY BLUEBERRY NIGHTS

During scenes of Jeremy (Jude Law) and Elizabeth (Norah Jones) getting acquainted in **My Blueberry Nights**, Chang cut to extreme closeups of Elizabeth's blueberry pie à la mode, the melting vanilla ice cream designed to convey the intense heat of romantic passion but also its transience. "We always love food," Chang says of himself and Wong. "We wanted to do a whole movie about food, and Wong hired a really good chef to cater every meal in the film. It was really delicious, but somehow we didn't end up doing it."

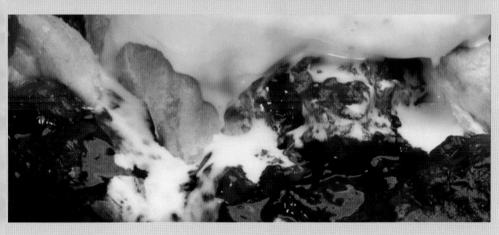

this film. Usually I try not to focus on the course of action; I focus on human behavior, and the course should arise from the behavior. With **In the Mood for Love**, I wanted to simply express the characters' behavior, rather than spelling out what they're thinking or saying. I tried to cut out anything that would suggest a narrative development and instead just focus on the hands, or the feet, or the back of Maggie Cheung's dress. I don't like to exaggerate things; I prefer very subtle feelings to overstated ones, and somehow **In the Mood for Love** allowed me to do that. It's a portrait of daily life. Yet somehow, the pacing of the whole film still managed to be fast. I didn't want the viewer to really linger on any emotions or any particular frame—the idea was to give you something and then quickly pull out.

2046 (2004) was a very ambiguous continuation of **In the Mood for Love**. We spent more than five years in production, but it only took three months to edit, which is not that long, relatively speaking. And it was extremely difficult to edit, because Wong had shot a lot of different scenes for the different storylines. The structure was incredibly loose—I could add a few scenes to one story, or cut a few scenes from another story. Emotionally, it was a very difficult film to pin down.

We didn't want to exaggerate the connection between **2046** and **In the Mood for Love** too much. Maggie's appearance in **2046** is very brief; either you see it or you don't. And it doesn't matter either way. It's just a memory of a woman from before. Tony's character is projecting all these feelings onto all these different women. We like ambiguity.

When I'm editing for performance, I try to get the best bits and pieces from each shot. So I have to remember the takes very clearly. When Wong is shooting, every take changes a little bit, whether it's the camera angle or the way he directs Tony to act. If he gives me ten takes, all ten will be different. It's good for me to have a variety of options to choose from, but it's a tedious if ultimately rewarding job. We're both friends with Tony and we know him too well, so →

IN THE MOOD FOR LOVE

For this film Chang decided on a subtle, almost perversely withholding editorial approach unique even in Wong's oeuvre. Favoring shots that provided only a partial or obscured view of events, Chang focused on closeups of hands clasping, cigarettes being lighted and meals being eaten, cutting them together with little regard for concrete narrative. "I wanted to simply express the characters' behavior, rather than spelling out what they're thinking or saying," he says.

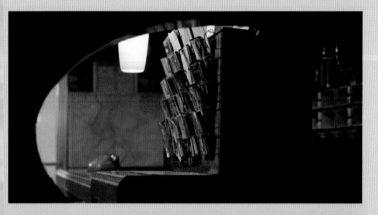

Delayed gratification

Not unlike Terrence Malick, Wong Kar-wai has developed a reputation for being so indecisive and unhurried in his methods that a single production can take years to complete. Wong's films are truly discovered in the cutting room, as one can glean from their elliptical and convulsive editorial rhythms. Yet if the director has been known to linger, Chang is accustomed to making up for lost time, working quickly and often under intense deadline pressure—particularly on two occasions when Wong kept audiences at the Cannes Film Festival waiting until the last minute.

In the Mood for Love (2000): Wong's heartsick memory piece was barely completed in time for its Cannes world premiere, screening on the final day of the festival with neither a title nor a complete sound mix. "We didn't talk, we didn't rush people, we just got it done—with very little sleep," Chang recalls. "We were under strain, but we tried not to show it. We are really cool people."

2046 (2004): This quasi-sequel to **In the Mood for Love** set a record for Cannes tardiness, missing two scheduled daytime screenings and finally arriving mere hours before its black-tie evening gala, according to *Variety*. After the festival, Wong and Chang spent another four months tinkering with the film before release, finalizing visual effects, adjusting the soundtrack and adding some footage, resulting in a final version four minutes longer than the 123-minute cut that premiered at Cannes.

SHADOWBOXER
Director Lee Daniels hired Chang to edit **Shadowboxer** on the basis of Chang's work on **In the Mood for Love**, though the final cut of Daniels' bizarre assassin-world thriller turned out to be much more straightforward—and rather different from Chang's original cut. "This film struck me as having a really weird story, and I felt it would be more effective with more raw, basic cuts, as in a Pasolini film. But they must have thought it wouldn't be commercial enough, and that the cross-cutting would make it more energetic."

for every performance I try to find something different from his work in previous films.

I'm always interested in working with different directors and trying something new, so when Lee Daniels called me about his new film, **Shadowboxer** (2005), I agreed to take it on. Lee had liked my work on **In the Mood for Love**, and he said he wanted something similar. But when I saw the rushes, I thought, wow this is completely different from **In the Mood for Love**. Maybe Lee likes the subtlety in my editing, but I can't do something like that with this film; it's just too different.

I edited the film in Hong Kong, and after I did the first cut I went to New York. Lee and I discussed every scene and made a few changes. After I left, they ended up altering the structure of the film even more, by adding a lot of cross-cutting between parallel scenes. I didn't think it should be done that way; it's too much cross-cutting. This film struck me as having a really weird story, and I felt it would be more effective with more raw, basic cuts, as in a Pasolini film. But they must have thought it wouldn't be commercial enough, and that the cross-cutting would make it more energetic, more interesting to look at. But it's okay. The director is the person who has the final say.

Right now Wong and I are working on **The**

Grandmasters, which features a lot of martial-arts sequences. I find that fight scenes are the easiest kind to edit, because there's a clear continuation of action to follow. They're usually filmed in very quick, short shots—a punch is followed by a cut, and the next shot will be whatever the guy punched at. So it's just a continuation of action until it comes to the end; it's easy. But I might play around with the timing and the speed, or I might use abstraction to prolong the moment by cutting away to something that has nothing to do with the action.

Every time I begin work on production design or editing, I feel very vulnerable and insecure. I never know what to do at first; each film is like a new thing to me. At that point I know I need to try a lot of different things, and then maybe one day, I'll get a very unusual feeling and start to follow it, and that's usually a good sign for the film. But that initial period of searching can be very difficult. Martin Scorsese says that every time he makes a movie, he feels as if he's starting all over from scratch. I know exactly how he feels. As fun as it is, you still feel enormous pressure, because you're always trying to do something you haven't done before.

2046

It took Chang three months to edit **2046**—not a long time in the context of a shoot that took more than five years, though the editor concedes it was a difficult process. The primary challenge was to strike the right balance, less structural than emotional, among the multiple storylines centered around the main character and the different women passing through his life (played by Zhang Ziyi, Gong Li and Faye Wong), as well as the science-fiction thread (featuring Takuya Kimura and Faye Wong).

Liao Ching-sung

"As a young man, I was obsessed with the beauty of editing. I loved how great editing could allow stories to be told so simply, succinctly, and with such beautiful rhythm and feeling, just by connecting a few shots."

As a boy growing up in Wanhua, the oldest district in Taipei, Liao Ching-sung was not only an avid moviegoer but also an amateur projectionist, building his own projectors using broken lenses from his local theater. His interest in cinema led him to study editing at Taiwan's Central Motion Picture Corporation in the early 1970s, where he apprenticed himself to Wang Jin-chen, eventually assisting Wang on Shan-his Ting's classic World War II epic **Everlasting Glory** (1975).

It was also at CMPC that Liao met fellow filmmaking aspirant Hou Hsiao-hsien, initiating a nearly four-decade collaboration that spans the entirety of Hou's oeuvre, from early features such as **The Boys From Fengkuei** (1983) and mid-career works **In the Hands of a Puppet Master** (1993) and **Flowers of Shanghai** (1998), to such recent films as **Café Lumière** (2003) and **Flight of the Red Balloon** (2007). Considered a key figure in Taiwanese cinema in his own right, and also active in the wider Chinese-language film industry, Liao also edited Edward Yang's **The Terrorizers** (1986), Yee Chih-yen's **Blue Gate Crossing** (2002), Wang Xiaoshuai's **Beijing Bicycle** (2001) and Jie Lu's **Courthouse on Horseback** (2006).

Liao Ching-sung

❝ Some editors like to think of themselves as God. They think, "Because I'm editing this film, I have the power to determine what kind of life it's supposed to take on. What people see is whatever I want them to see." I feel a movie has a life of its own. The moment something is captured on celluloid, it's already taken on a new life. It's like a baby, and despite your best plans and efforts, ultimately you can't control its personality and temperament once it's born. So it is with editing. It takes keen observation and intimate communication with a film in order to understand it and subsequently help give it the life it needs through editing.

Sometimes the end result takes on a new form that surprises me, a form that I did not anticipate or plan for at all. When I edit, I simply follow the emotion of the film and make intuitive decisions that I think are faithful to its spirit. Hou Hsiao-hsien and I are in absolute agreement on this. His hope is always for a film to take on a life of its own, to flourish in a way that's unique and unexpected, yet faithful to its original vision and spirit. Cinema is fluid and alive. It's not as though there are only so many ways to direct or edit a movie. The possibilities are rich and endless.

As a young man, I was obsessed with the beauty of editing. I loved how great editing could allow stories to be told so simply, succinctly, and with such beautiful rhythm and feeling, just by connecting a few shots. I loved seeing shots transformed. The transition between shots, the feeling of transformation and visual excitement that editing could create, was mesmerizing to me.

I read a lot of film theory and criticism when I was growing up, and I was eager to tell stories. My father had passed away when I was nine, and my mother was very protective of me. As a result, I was very introverted, and storytelling became my means of self-expression. Growing up, I would watch TV series like **Combat!**, **The Avengers** and **Night Gallery**, where Steven Spielberg got his start, and write down their shot lists and analyze them with a red pen on the side and try to figure out why the scenes were put together the way they were.

THE TERRORIZERS
While Edward Yang drew up a meticulous storyboard for **The Terrorizers** (1986), Liao Ching-sung wound up completely changing the order of his shots within each scene. "I thought he was being a little too explicit and obvious with the way he was telling the story," Liao recalls. "I edited the film based on what I thought the audience was thinking and feeling, and I would try to communicate with them through every shot." While Yang didn't take too kindly to these changes initially, Liao insisted on his choices, "albeit in a very, very gentle and polite way."

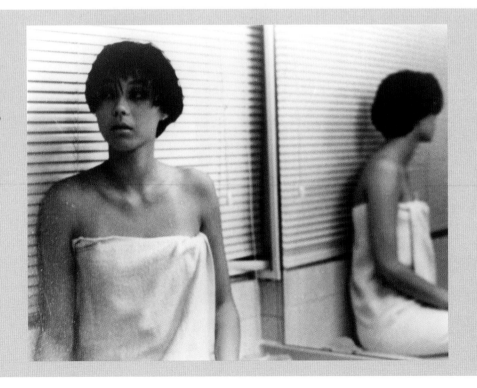

At the end of 1973, I entered Central Motion Picture Cooperation's newly founded, three-month-long technical training program, specializing in editing. By the third month of the CMPC program, you would already be working directly with a professional as their apprentice. That's how I received most of my early training and experience. I would observe these professional technicians at work. At the time, we were still using hand-crank viewers, and we had to manually rewind everything—this was well before the age of Moviola. They would give me scenes to edit and offer me direct feedback. "This part is too fast," or "this part is too slow," etc. They were used to editing what were essentially silent films with no synchronized sound, and they would use their hands and bodies to measure the length of the film strip and cut certain scenes.

I remember the first time a "real" scene was given to me to edit. It was a fight scene from **Spy Ring Kokuryuaki** (1976, Ting Shan-hsi). It was something that nowadays would probably take me no more than ten minutes to edit, but →

In their time

The 1982 rise of New Taiwanese Cinema, also known as the Taiwanese New Wave, brought with it a number of technological innovations long since taken for granted by filmmakers outside the region. Along with fellow key New Wave figures such as Hou Hsiao-hsien and Edward Yang, Liao played a crucial role in implementing such techniques in his native cinema.

Coverage: When Yang was filming his contribution to the seminal 1982 four-part anthology film **In Our Time**, he presented Liao with a detailed storyboard for a scene of a boy riding a bicycle. "I told him, 'Just shoot everything, shoot from all the angles you want, and we can worry about how the scene should look later,'" Liao says. "This way, he wouldn't have to worry about connecting the shots and making them flow while he was on set. He could just concentrate on directing the performances."

Master shots: "People didn't used to do master shots in Taiwan, but we started doing them. If you have a scene with two reverse angles, it's enormously difficult to have to break up the shots and shoot them separately. So why not just do two master shots and edit them together later?" Liao says. "Of course, what I didn't know was how hard it would be to edit a scene with two master shots, especially for films without synchronized sound. If you messed up the first shot in the editing stage, everything else would be off, like a chain reaction. I was asking for trouble."

Synchronized sound: Hou and Liao helped inaugurate the use of synchronized sound, using a Sony TCD5 cassette recorder to capture sound on location; Liao would then refer to the tape as a blueprint in the cutting room. "Even though the sound was on a separate tape and not synchronized, at least when I edited I knew what the characters were saying when I edited the scenes. I now had a point of reference." Until that point, most Taiwanese movies had been dubbed using professional voice actors. In pursuit of greater realism, the New Wave directors began having their onscreen actors record their own dialogue.

"Cutting a film is like building a ladder for the audience... If you miss a step, the audience will fall off and end up somewhere you didn't intend."

at the time, it took me roughly three days. I worked very hard and applied all the theoretical knowledge I had accumulated over the years to editing that one scene. When I finally played the finished footage for myself on the big screen—I will never forget this—it was the most poorly assembled thing I had ever seen in my entire life. Everything was off. It was a great personal disappointment. I learned right then and there that it was utterly useless to only know theories. I had to practice.

Before the advent of New Taiwanese Cinema in the early 1980s, the films director Hou and I were making were rather commercial in nature. We would always get tired with what we were doing, and we would wonder to ourselves, "Why do stories have to be told this way?" We were very dissatisfied. At the time I loved hanging out at the Taipei Film Archive, and one day in the early 1980s I saw that they were doing a festival showcasing classic French films. I went and devoured everything. I spent days at the Film Archive, watching film after film. It was my first time seeing films such as **Last Year at Marienbad** (1961), **Hiroshima Mon Amour** (1959) and **Breathless** (1960). I recommended them to Hou, and he thought they were fantastic. He saw them right before he went off to shoot **The Boys From Fengkuei** (1983), and they ended up influencing the way he made that film.

Around the same time, I began to edit films based on the emotional logic of the characters and their story, rather than on the traditional logic of storytelling. I was moving toward a more poetic approach. As an editor and therefore an author on a film, I needed to figure out what role I would play in this dynamic interplay between myself and the audience. Should I do what Hollywood filmmakers do—direct the audience, tell them how to feel and therefore be very visible in the process as an author—or should I let the audience members feel for themselves and work things out on their own?

Editing involves a great deal of deliberation. In the past, I would edit something and come back to it a few days later and be surprised at what I

had done. "What was I thinking? Why did I make those decisions?" I'd ask myself. To avoid that, I've since developed the habit of regularly questioning myself whenever I edit and make decisions. It's not an easy thing to do; it takes practice.

Another thing that requires practice is the ability to "forget"—to watch something you've edited as if you've never seen it before. An inability to be flexible and see things from other perspectives, from other conceptual viewpoints, is deadly when it comes to art. If you don't practice the art of forgetting, you can't come to your film with a fresh mindset and consistently arrive at the audience's viewpoint. Cutting a film is like building a ladder for the audience. You want to prepare the steps carefully. If you miss a step, the audience will fall off and end up somewhere you didn't intend.

Edward Yang had become very good friends with director Hou and me, and he asked me to edit **The Terrorizers** (1986) around the same time Hou was making **Dust in the Wind** (1987). Edward had a background in engineering, and so his shots were very meticulous and precise. He had a large white board at home on which he'd draw up flow charts for his movies. Nonetheless, I changed his shot order completely, because I thought he was being a little too explicit and obvious with the way he was telling the story. I edited the film based on what I thought the audience was thinking and feeling, and I would try to communicate with them through every shot. When you watch **The Terrorizers**, the idea is for you to feel as though every shot is creating a sense of dread and tension. This was especially difficult because the film had multiple storylines, and I needed to be very delicate in my approach and avoid any false note that would disrupt the film's overall flow.

For four days straight, Edward would review the edited footage and ask me, "Why did you cut it like that?" I would insist on my choices, albeit in a very, very, gentle and polite way. I still kept all his shots; I would just change the order in which they appeared in a given scene. Edward finally →

FLOWERS OF SHANGHAI

Liao didn't know at first how to transition between the many long takes in Hou Hsiao-hsien's **Flowers of Shanghai**, a problem he solved using a simple, but dramatically effective, fade effect. "The fade-ins and fade-outs in the film happen very slowly, as if you are watching a play," he says. "I reviewed each scene from beginning to end, over and over again, to figure out the precise moments at which to fade out and bring in the next scene. The scene fades out and disappears as the emotion of the scene is also dissipating."

> ### "I didn't care about traditional storytelling logic at all. You don't need to explain everything to the audience."

gave me his trust and support, and let me finish **The Terrorizers**, though we never did work together again. I regret the fact that he didn't let me edit **A Brighter Summer Day** (1991). I wouldn't have minded even if he didn't end up using my cut. At least let me take a stab at it!

Hou Hsiao-hsien and I hit it off right from the start. We liked working together and were kindred spirits. The collaboration has now lasted 37 years. We didn't realize we had been together this long until we did the math recently. It honestly still feels like yesterday when we first started working together. Our relationship is unique: We grew up together, so to speak, in the film industry. He's been my teacher, friend and competitor, and now we are like brothers. I love the movies he makes; they are the kinds of movies that I'd want to make as a director. Helping Hou complete his work is a way for me to fulfill my own deepest wishes and creative desires.

When I first started editing **A City of Sadness** (1989), scenes would go missing randomly in the editing room. I'd be working on the tenth scene and notice that the fifth scene had somehow disappeared. I became anxious and brought it up with Hou, who told me, "I don't feel like having those scenes anymore, so I got rid of them." He thought the film was becoming cinematically verbose, that the scenes were annoying and explained or showed too much. I said, "Director, you can't do this. The scenes are not connecting. If we keep doing this, the movie will be a mess. It will be incomprehensible!"

Knowing Hou was set on his strategy, I started to edit with the mindset of a Tang Dynasty poet, using the same kind of emotional, poetic logic to assemble the film. I realized that there were, in fact, many things the audience didn't need to know, things I could just get rid of. In the opening scene, for example, I tried to create a mood that was faithful to the era immediately after World War II. My editing strategy was all about conjuring the atmosphere, the air of that time period. The transitions between all the scenes in the film were purposely edited to resemble the transitions in traditional Chinese poetry, predicated upon and unified by the same emotional logic. I also used the poetic technique of reversal a lot, placing scenes out of chronology. I didn't care about traditional

THE PUPPETMASTER

Hou's films are often noted for their long takes, a technique that was taken to a particular extreme with **The Puppetmaster.** In this documentary-fiction hybrid that chronicles the life of the Taiwanese puppet artist Li Tien-lu, the camera often lingers for minutes on a landscape, an interview with Li or a closeup of one of the traveling puppet troupe's productions. "We purposely used extreme long takes to generate an air of authentic reality," says Liao. "It's a narrative film that documents reality, that captures and restores a sense of real life."

storytelling logic at all. You don't need to explain everything to the audience. As long as the entire film is sustained by the same emotional, poetic logic, it would be fine. The audience would understand it.

In **A City of Sadness**, the camera doesn't really move. Instead, a poetic rhythm emerges from the shots and the way they are combined and connected. But for something like **The Puppetmaster** (1993), we purposely used extremely long takes to generate an air of authentic reality; it's sort of like a narrative film that documents reality, that captures and restores a sense of real life. Whereas **A City of Sadness** is poetic, I'd say **The Puppetmaster** is more "real." We used long takes to the extreme on this.

Beginning with **Good Men, Good Women** (1995), Hou started to move his camera again. My personal view is that he had reached the limit with the quiet, unobtrusive kind of invisibility that's typical of his earlier films. Whereas before he was a quiet observer—offering sensitive insight from a distance—now he wanted to move around and look everywhere, with camera pans and all. It's still naturalistic, but in a different way.

I had more work to do because I now needed to take into consideration the movement of the camera, the movement of the people, what's happening in the physical space of a scene, etc. People look at these films and hardly notice the cuts; they think the films are barely edited. What they don't know is that sometimes it'd take me hours to review a scene just so I could find the right moment to make my cut. The takes are all very long. It's funny; as more time was needed to be spent on editing, the role of the editor became less noticeable.

I didn't know how to edit **Flowers of Shanghai** (1998) at first. The film was all long takes. We didn't have any exterior scenes that could be used for transitions, and I was not inclined to use closeups for those purposes. I tried the fade effect just to experiment, and the effect was beautiful beyond my expectations. The fade-ins and fade-outs in the film happen very slowly, as if you are watching a play. I became very excited; I felt I had found a technique that would allow the audience to calmly and objectively watch the story unfold. I reviewed each scene from beginning to end, over and over again, to figure out the precise moments at →

THREE TIMES

Hou's 2005 omnibus **Three Times** tells three love stories, each of which deploys an editing style appropriate to its particular era. The first film, "A Time for Love," unfolds in a series of pool halls in 1966, and is cut in an even, gentle manner that balances long takes and a gently moving camera. The second film, "A Time for Freedom," set in an upscale brothel in 1911, evokes silent movies with occasional inter-titles. The third film, the contemporary-set "A Time for Youth," represents a loose jumble of images and impressions, with frequent cutaways to closeups of cell phones and computer screens.

CAFÉ LUMIÈRE

This film proved quite a logistical challenge for Liao, not least because Hou and his crew spent a long time getting all the different train-related shots they wanted. It took 14 train rides just to get the shot in which Yoko (Hitoto Yo) is visible on one train in the foreground, with her friend Hajime (Asano Tadanobu) visible on another train passing in the background. "This made editing all the more painful, because in order to complete a scene like that, I had to assemble footage from the 14 takes we did," Liao says.

which to fade out and bring in the next scene. The scene fades out and disappears as the emotion of the scene is also dissipating.

When I'm editing, I will keep watching the film over and over again. I simply watch and receive, and then I am able to communicate with it and understand the kind of life it has. To watch a film instinctually like this means not bringing in any judgment, analysis, preconceived ideas or ideology to bear upon it. Remember that the film is speaking to you, not the other way around.

Editing is about unleashing the soul of a film. I very much agree with the way Auguste Rodin put it: He needed to find the soul of a rock and unleash it so the rock could flourish and be molded into the work of art it could be. A film is even more complex than a rock. A film is alive. You need to understand it intimately and experience it deeply, and then you will be ready to nurture it, unleash its potential, and give it the life that it truly needs.

Conducted and translated by Eugene Suen.

Hervé de Luze

"Editing, for me, is primarily a matter of instinct rather than adherence to any particular rule of grammar. I don't know if it can be taught. It's something you have to feel."

Hervé de Luze was ten years old when he first became interested in filmmaking, spurred in part by his father, who worked at a film distribution company and often took his son to see movies for free at theaters on the Champs-Élysées. After spending a year working with the famed film archivist Henri Langlois at the Cinémathèque Française in Paris, where he immersed himself in the glories of silent cinema, de Luze produced short TV documentaries before beginning his career as a picture editor, specializing initially in underground and experimental cinema.

De Luze edited eight films for the late producer-director Claude Berri, including **Jean de Florette** (1986, with Arlette Langmann and Noelle Boisson), **Manon of the Spring** (1986, with Geneviève Louveau) and **Uranus** (1990). He has also enjoyed a lengthy collaboration with Roman Polanski, having cut each of his films from **Pirates** (1986) to **The Ghost** (2010), and recently cut the director's **Carnage** (2011), adapted from the play **God of Carnage**. De Luze received an Academy Award nomination for editing Polanski's Holocaust drama **The Pianist** (2002) and has won three César Awards for editing—for Alain Resnais' **Same Old Song** (1997), Guillaume Canet's **Tell No One** (2006) and Polanski's **The Ghost**. His other credits include Agnieszka Holland's **To Kill a Priest** (1988), Arnaud Desplechin's **Esther Kahn** (2000) and Agnès Jaoui's **The Taste of Others** (2000).

Hervé de Luze

I spent one year watching at least one silent movie a day while attending Henri Langlois' lectures at the Cinémathèque Française. That was my film school and it was, I think, the best one. I saw a lot of movies from different countries and movements, from Italian neorealism and Soviet cinema to the French New Wave and the golden age of American musicals, but I learned the most about editing from silent movies such as Murnau's **Sunrise** (1927) and **Nosferatu** (1922), Fritz Lang's **Destiny** (1921) and **Metropolis** (1927), among many others.

Most of the silent movies were in German, which ended up being a great lesson for me: without sound or an ability to read the language, I had to focus on the picture. Henri would screen ten-minute reels of film, and beforehand he would spend ten minutes explaining to us what we were about to see. There were all these different films screening one after another, and yet because of Henri's explanations, they were so clear, and you could understand everything. I've never met a guy able to put together and pull apart films as well as Henri.

When I started, of course, everything was on film stock—16mm for low budget and experimental movies, and 35mm for the biggest productions. Cutting on film required a different approach; you had to think a lot before making any cut, because every cut was very visible. You could feel it much more than you do now in digital. There was also the noise of the splice, and if you cut something too short, any extension would be very visible and noisy, too. If you thought the storytelling was too clumsy or boring, it would need to be changed and rebuilt, and to do that you would have to write out the new order of scenes on paper.

Now, of course, you can just test it immediately because it's so easy to do. Digital editing is a fantastic synthetic tool. It allows you to add music to scenes, mix dialogue and other sound—all those things that were more complicated to do before, and which are so important to the editing process. What's great in digital systems is the flexibility and speed; because you are able to try so many different things, your decisions stem more from what you see onscreen than from what

JEAN DE FLORETTE

When de Luze came aboard Claude Berri's **Jean de Florette** (which he co-edited with Arlette Langmann and Noelle Boisson), the film was about two hours and 25 minutes. De Luze managed to trim it down to two hours, removing material he thought was extraneous while restoring about 30 scenes that had been cut from the picture. "For me, those scenes were very interesting and provided a sense of time passing that was not conveyed very effectively in the first cut," de Luze says. "For that kind of an epic movie, you have to show the seasons changing."

you think. In the past, you would hesitate before making an inappropriate cut and wait for good ideas to come. Now, you make an inappropriate cut and it helps you to find the right one.

Digital editing also allows you to summarize the entire film very quickly, so that you have a complete vision of the story based on the images, not the script. When I first read a screenplay, I develop a precise idea of the story and the characters, but I know that it may evolve a lot during shooting. So I never read the screenplay again just before starting to edit. I don't have any clear plan before I get the first dailies.

Once shooting starts, the "second writing" begins. From here on, you have to write with pictures. Rushes dictate the shape of each scene. This is when you see the director's point of view, when you understand how he sees the scene and what he wants to say. My first step is always to make an assembly, alone—a rough cut that's close to the ideas I feel in the dailies. And then I work with the director in the cutting room. Since the film is the director's vision, I am very much inclined to trust him or her on continuity and →

A French twist

The sense of freewheeling creative experimentation that proliferated during the French New Wave was especially apparent in the films' often audacious editing techniques. Here are three New Wave masters whose earliest cinematic doodles had a lasting impact on the language of cinema.

Jean-Luc Godard: The director's bold, playful use of jump cuts in **Breathless** (1960) remains perhaps the definitive emblem of the French New Wave's far-reaching stylistic impact, shattering the illusion of continuity as well as the viewer's complacency.

Alain Resnais: Hiroshima Mon Amour (1959) and **Last Year at Marienbad** (1961) not only tackled a defiantly non-linear structure but made inventive use of flashback inserts to evoke the restless, mercurial nature of human memory.

François Truffaut: After ending **The 400 Blows** (1959) on a haunting freeze-frame, Truffaut made **Shoot the Piano Player** (1960), a supremely inventive gangster picture that deployed a wild panoply of editing techniques, its disjunctive rhythms underscoring its unusual shifts in tone, genre and style.

THE PIANIST

De Luze was skeptical initially of Roman Polanski's decision to tackle **The Pianist**, an adaptation of a memoir by Holocaust survivor Wladyslaw Szpilman. "The challenge for me in the cutting room was how to account for the passing of time," he says, noting that the second half of the film was essentially a drawn-out study of isolation, with Szpilman hiding out in a series of apartments in the Warsaw Ghetto. De Luze's strategy was to keep the style plain and grounded, and to trust Adrien Brody's performance to maintain a hold on the audience's attention.

choice of takes, because they know what is good and what is not. The most important thing for an editor to do is to remain the first spectator throughout the process of editing, to be able to constantly bring to the director the spectator's point of view, even after dozens of screenings.

Of course, one of the great things about editing is that you get to work on different films with different directors, so it's never routine. Roman Polanski, for example, always concentrates on the accuracy and precision of the storytelling. Meaning is crucial, and the motivations of the characters have to be clear. The decisions are always dramatic, never aesthetic. Nothing is gratuitous, and you have to know why you make a cut. Roman loves editing because it's the moment when the film takes shape.

The last scene of **Bitter Moon** (1992), the New Year's Eve party on the boat, was an editing

nightmare. Technically it was very complicated. We had these very long, Steadicam shots with a lot of people in the frame and a band playing in sync all through the scene. Amid this huge mess, you had to follow the four characters in a dramatic crescendo leading up to the final tragedy. I think I dragged that scene behind me all through the editing process, for about ten months. Before each screening, I would tell Roman, "The scene is not ready yet!" And he would answer, "I know!" Fortunately, by the time of the last projection, just before the final mix, somehow that scene came together very naturally and quickly.

One of my most difficult films to cut for Roman was **The Pianist** (2002). I remember reading Wladyslaw Szpilman's book and saying to Roman, "What are you going to do with this? It's impossible, it's not a film." And then I read the script, which was a good script, but I was worried

Arena Films/Caméra One/France 2 Cinéma/Vega Film/Greenpoint Films

SAME OLD SONG

During the extended cocktail-party sequence in **Same Old Song**, Alain Resnais came up with the playful idea of superimposing shots of jellyfish over the dissolves from one scene to another. "It's funny because it has apparently nothing to do with the party, but at the same time, you can read it as an expression of what the characters feel and the relationships among them," Hervé de Luze says. "Alain has a very childish, innocent sense of humor." The director made use of a similar if less bizarre transitional effect in **Private Fears in Public Places**, in which scenes are divided by a quick dissolve to a shot of falling snow.

that it might be too boring. The challenge for me in the cutting room was how to account for the passing of time, particularly in the second half of the film, when you have a guy locked alone in a flat for months, looking down at the street where nothing is happening. The audience must not be bored, and yet any cinematic trick, any expression of skill or virtuosity, would have made the film seem phony and unreal. It had to remain simple and everyday-like. I don't know how we managed to do it, but we did. You have a different relationship with the director on each film, and while Roman and I were quite close already, we became even closer on **The Pianist**, because it was so intimate and so personal.

Working with Claude Berri was quite different. He worked in a more popular style, and he was anxious to be liked and anxious to entertain. Editing wasn't his favorite step in the →

MANON DES SOURCES

One of the most wrenching scenes in this film—in which Ugolin (Daniel Auteuil) confesses his love for Manon (Emmanuelle Béart) in front of the entire village—gave Berri so much trouble that he suggested they scrap it, to de Luze's horror. The editor salvaged the scene by keeping Auteuil in the frame as much as possible and cutting elsewhere only when absolutely necessary. "The emotion was so intense, thanks to Daniel's performance, that the scene was still extremely moving in the end," he says.

moviemaking process; and most of the time he would let me do it on my own; he preferred to speak about the editing after each screening. He kept me close, though. When he shot **Uranus** (1990), it was his first time working with a monitor-TV combo, and he wanted me "fanatically" with him at all times. He even asked me to help him prepare the shots. Because of all the time I spent on the set, putting the rough cut together went so much faster than it otherwise would have. The assembly took about a week.

We editors are very close to our directors in France, much more so than we are to the producers. We're paid by the producers, but we are loyal to the director always. Sometimes it's even difficult to work with two directors in France. There's a kind of jealousy; Roman doesn't like me to work with other directors. Ironically, I first met Claude through Roman. I had come for three weeks to replace an assistant on **Tess** (1979), just before the film's European release. Two months later, I was called back because Claude, who was producing **Tess**, wanted to shorten it for the US release. Roman was so pleased with my work that he eventually asked me to cut his next film, **Pirates** (1986).

Because of my commitment to **Pirates**, I ended up starting very late on editing **Manon des Sources** (1986). When I began, Claude told me he was having problems with the key scene in the film—when the main character, Ugolin (Daniel Auteuil), confesses his love for Manon in front of the whole village—and that he thought we should skip it. I was horrified by the idea. When I looked at the first day's worth of shooting, they had focused only on Daniel, and his performance was so moving that I got goosebumps looking at the dailies. But on the second day's worth of shooting, they had decided to go in an entirely different direction, and nothing in the scene was matching. I ended up focusing mostly on the first day's footage of Daniel; I had to use the second day for other parts of the scene, but the emotion was so intense, thanks to Daniel's performance, that the scene was still extremely moving in the end. →

TELL NO ONE

Guillaume Canet's disregard for conventional cinema grammar in **Tell No One** provided de Luze with a fascinating departure from his typically precise, methodical work for Polanski. The film's central setpiece—a chase sequence in which police pursue the hero, Dr. Alex Beck (François Cluzet), across a busy motorway—required de Luze to cut very quickly among several handheld cameras, using a rough-and-ready style and never returning to the same angle. "It was difficult to cut because it wasn't meant to be a brilliant stunt. It was from the point of view of a simple man, a doctor, not a superhero."

I think we editors owe everything to actors. The editing of a film cannot be good if the actors aren't. They give you the tempo of the scenes, the feelings of the characters. They tell the story; we just put in the accents. When you work on a film where the performances are all great, it's like eating caviar at every meal: pleasure, pleasure, pleasure. The best editing is effortless; you're just carried along by the performances. Already I'm excited to cut **Carnage**, because the cast is so great. And I remember in **The Pianist**, when I was cutting the scene with Adrien Brody playing the piano for Thomas Kretschmann, I felt I was useless. It was so great in the dailies already.

Alain Resnais asked me to do **Same Old Song** (1997) because of his admiration for Roman Polanski, which is ironic because Alain's style is very peculiar. He does not think the same way as many people. He's a poet, and his ideas are very close to those of the Surrealist movement, and he uses collage, often combining shots that don't match, in order to tell the story and arouse the feelings. When you work with him, it's always an appointment with surprise. Imagination rules.

For instance, in **Same Old Song**, when the transparent jellyfish are superimposed over the cocktail-party scene, it's funny because it has apparently nothing to do with the party, but at the same time, you can read it as an expression of what the characters feel and the relationships among them. But when you ask Alain about it, he says, "I don't know." He never helps you. You have the right to think whatever you want.

Alain doesn't shoot very much, but he's very precise. Vague, yet precise. He never tells you what to do; you're supposed to figure it out from his direction and the way he's shooting. Everything he gives you is useful. With Alain you're throwing out two or three shots in a film, no more. Also, he's able to film shots that are very, very long in terms of duration, but within the workings of this shot, you have closeups as well as wide shots—it's like it's already cut, even though it's one shot. It's fantastic. On **Same Old Song** the number of shots was around 300, which is nothing, but there might be the equivalent of 50 shots in one long shot.

Still, it was quite a challenge to cut the ending of **Wild Grass** (2009), which is almost absurd. I remember staring at the various shots of this sequence, in complete disorder, wondering whether they could mean something. When

WILD GRASS

In the final sequence of Resnais' **Wild Grass**, a plane crashes, the camera tracks backward through a forest (and possibly through time), swoops over some ancient-looking rock formations and eventually comes to rest in the bedroom of a young girl, who asks her mother, "Mommy, if I come back as a kitty, may I munch on kitty nibbles?" The sequence made no more sense to de Luze in the cutting room than it does to the viewer. "I remember staring at the various shots of this sequence, in complete disorder, wondering whether they could mean something," de Luze recalls. "When you've finished editing a scene like that, you feel as if you've been carried along by a stream that you do not control. It's very difficult to explain afterward why you did one thing and not the other."

you've finished editing a scene like that, you feel as if you've been carried along by a stream that you do not control. It's very difficult afterward to explain why you did one thing and not the other.

The only rule in editing is that emotion trumps every rule in editing. That is the lesson of Orson Welles' **Othello** (1952), which is a masterpiece particularly in terms of its editing: it's amazing how Welles chooses to tell the story, which is made up of so many different bits, and has four different actresses playing Desdemona and only one strong character in the end. Yet he makes you experience the feelings of the characters so deeply. Editing, for me, is primarily a matter of instinct rather than adherence to any particular rule of grammar. I don't know if it can be taught. It's something you have to feel.

Barbara McLean

Film editing is often hailed as one of the few jobs in showbiz that has afforded a great many opportunities for women—a truism that can be accepted or refuted, depending on whether one places more weight on statistics (going strictly by the numbers, men still dwarf women in the field), or on the daunting caliber of work from the likes of Margaret Booth, Verna Fields, Anne Bauchens, Anne Voase Coates, Dede Allen, Thelma Schoonmaker and so on.

Certainly the profession would have been a less inclusive one without the pioneering career of Barbara McLean, who, like Booth, was one of the first women to work as a film editor in Hollywood. Born in 1903 in Palisades Park, N.J., she grew up working in the film laboratory of her father, Charles Pollut, and became an assistant editor at First National Studio before going to work at 20th Century Pictures (before it merged with Fox Film Corporation in 1935). She received her first feature-editing credit on Gregory La Cava's **Gallant Lady** (1933) and received the first of seven Academy Award nominations for editing Richard Boleslawski's **Les Misérables** (1935).

McLean is particularly notable for having served as chief editor at 20th Century Fox, a post she held for more than 30 years until her retirement in 1969. During this time, she not only maintained editorial oversight on all the studio's films, but served as the highly esteemed and closely trusted confidante of Fox head Darryl F. Zanuck, who often consulted "Bobby" in numerous aspects of filmmaking. Among her numerous noteworthy credits for the studio were Clarence Brown's **The Rains Came** (1939), John Ford's **Tobacco Road** (1941), George Cukor's **Winged Victory** (1944), Edmund Goulding's **Nightmare Alley** (1947), Elia Kazan's **Viva Zapata** (1952) and Michael Curtiz's **The Egyptian** (1954).

But McLean's longest and most prolific working relationship was with the director Henry King, and their nearly 20-year collaboration

01 The Song of Bernadette

02 Wilson

01

02

included such films as **The Country Doctor** (1936), **Lloyd's of London** (1936), **In Old Chicago** (1937), **Seventh Heaven** (1937), Alexander's **Ragtime Band** (1938), **The Song of Bernadette** (1943) and **Wilson** (1944), the now little-seen presidential biopic that finally scored her an Oscar after five nominations. According to *Daily Variety*, McLean "was overcome, flabbergasted and became almost unconscious as she heard her name announced" and "slept with her statuette under her pillow." Along with Michael Kahn and her protégé William H. Reynolds, McLean holds the record for most Academy Award nominations for film editing (seven).

Still, the Academy neglected to recognize some of McLean's most significant editorial accomplishments, among them **Twelve O'Clock High** (1949), King's World War II picture starring Gregory Peck, and Henry Koster's 1953 Biblical epic **The Robe**, the first picture to be released

in CinemaScope. She did receive an Oscar nomination for **All About Eve** (1950), the Joseph L. Mankiewicz classic that arguably holds up best among the 60 films she edited.

McLean was known for the seamlessness of her work, a quality much prized by the classical Hollywood tradition in which she thrived. "Good film editing is selecting the best of the film. Great film editing occurs when you begin with great pictures," she famously remarked in a Film Comment interview from the 1970s, by which point she had retired from 20th Century Fox due to the ailing health of her second husband, the director Robert D. Webb. McLean died in 1996, more than four decades after receiving her final editing credit on King's **Untamed**.

03

04

Angus Wall & Kirk Baxter

"Cutting movies can be such a lonely endeavor. Why not have a partner? I know when we're on the movie together, it's a lot more fun than when we're working individually."

Angus Wall began his entertainment career as an editor of music videos and commercials in the late 1980s before he and his wife, Linda Carlson, established Rock Paper Scissors, an editorial house based in Los Angeles. Wall's collaboration with David Fincher began when he designed the titles for the director's **Se7en** (1995), after which he served as editorial consultant on **Fight Club** (1999) and co-edited **Panic Room** (2002) with James Haygood. His other editing credits include Adam Collis' **Sunset Strip** (2000) and Mike Mills' **Thumbsucker** (2005).

Born and raised in Sydney, Australia, Kirk Baxter co-founded a commercial editing firm, Final Cut, before moving to Los Angeles and joining Rock Paper Scissors in 2004. He made his transition into features in 2007, serving as additional editor to Wall on Fincher's **Zodiac** (2007). The duo have since co-edited **The Curious Case of Benjamin Button** (2008) and **The Social Network** (2010), which earned them the Academy Award and ACE Eddie Award for best editing. They recently edited Fincher's English-language remake of **The Girl with the Dragon Tattoo** (2010).

Angus Wall & Kirk Baxter

ANGUS WALL I think editing is one of the few aspects of filmmaking where it can be really beneficial to have more than one person. But they have to be the right people, and it has to be a partnership based on generosity and graciousness, not on competition. I know there are directors who will put editors in competition, which can be very detrimental to the working relationship of the whole team. Kirk and I are incredibly lucky because we both work the same way; we're working toward a common goal, which is to illuminate the story, and we're working with a director, David Fincher, who is constructive as opposed to destructive.

KIRK BAXTER Nothing's personal with David. Well, everything's personal and nothing's personal. It's always about helping the movie, and I always say that David and the movie are one and the same thing. When he critiques your work, he's really critiquing himself, and he's striving to get the material to a place of perfection and simplicity. The work becomes really easy when that's kept in mind.

WALL People bring different things to a project. There is a mechanical nature to editing, which is essentially putting a scene together and selecting the best elements. But you always want to be in an environment where what you're bringing to the party, apart from that mechanical skill, is going to shine. David is so good at everybody else's jobs, you hope and pray, if you're working with him, that you're going to bring something of yourself to it.

BAXTER It's hard to beat David on the initial assembly within a scene. He shot it all, and he knew exactly what he was going for. So at first, we're just playing catch-up. But once the ball starts rolling and the scenes start getting joined together, that's when we start to love it.

ZODIAC

For **Zodiac** editor Angus Wall and additional editor Kirk Baxter, the challenge of David Fincher's procedural drama lay in forging a compelling narrative out of the raw factual data and minutiae concerning the Zodiac case. The killer's brutal attack on Bryan Hartnell (Patrick Scott Lewis) and Cecelia Shepard (Pell James) occurs within the first 30 minutes and is the last act of explicit violence in the film, which is largely devoted to documenting the investigations of cartoonist Robert Graysmith (Jake Gyllenhaal), David Toschi (Mark Ruffalo) and Paul Avery (Robert Downey Jr.).

Despite some pressure to excise scenes and bring down the running time, Fincher stuck to his guns; the eventual director's cut of **Zodiac** ran 162 minutes, just five minutes longer than the theatrical cut. "It was important to make sure that the film stayed true to the story," Wall notes. "It was all about the accumulation of detail."

> ## "The coverage on **The Social Network** appears to be pretty simple…It looks like meat and potatoes, but it's actually beef bourguignon."

WALL I'm probably going to misquote him, but Walter Murch says that when you stop seeing yourself in the work, that's when you're starting to get somewhere. Most of the time in David's movies, we're trying to get out of the way of the story. We're trying to let the audience get lost in the words and the performances. That's always our goal.

BAXTER David's work tends to be crafted in a way that's seamless, because he shoots enough coverage and is a big stickler for continuity, for not crossing the line unless it's really deliberate, and so on. For a guy who's known to be quite aggressive filmically, the laws of film are always being respected.

WALL The coverage on **The Social Network** (2010), for example, appears to be pretty simple. But if you look at those boardroom scenes in particular, the way they're staged and blocked is very sophisticated. But it's not showy. It looks like meat and potatoes, but it's actually beef bourguignon.

BAXTER I saw that come to fruition in the scene toward the end of the movie, when Mark Zuckerberg is on the phone with Sean Parker, who's at the police station. You have Mark on one side of the frame, talking, talking, talking, and then he swings in his chair to the other side of the frame. Then Sean comes in, doing a similar dance from one side of the frame to the next. And those shots seamlessly stitch together, so that the two are always on opposite sides of the frame when they're delivering their dialogue. It's so helpful, because David's blocked these things so that as soon as someone lands on one side of the frame, bang! You can cut instantly. He's so good. He gives you the material. And we're the ones who end up looking clever. →

THE SOCIAL NETWORK

Wall spent three weeks fine-cutting the opening
sequence of **The Social Network**, a six-minute, back-
and-forth fusillade of dialogue between Mark Zuckerberg
(Jesse Eisenberg) and Erica Albright (Rooney Mara) that
demanded cutting as rapid-fire yet precise as the actors'
delivery. He divided the scene into five sections and built
each one before stringing them together. "It was a very
important scene, because it set the tone for the rest of
the film," he says. "It's a bit of a warning shot over the
bow for the audience members, letting them know that
they're going to have to pay attention during this movie."

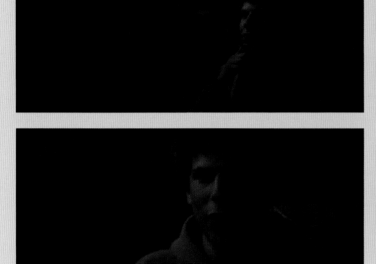

Columbia Pictures

WALL The opening scene of **The Social Network**
was a very, very fun scene to do, because it was
just two people, and there was nowhere for me as
an editor to hide. And there was no need to hide,
because the performances by Jesse Eisenberg
and Rooney Mara were so good. Plus, it was a
very important scene, because it set the tone for
the rest of the film—it's a bit of a warning shot
over the bow for the audience members, letting
them know that they're going to have to pay
attention during this movie.

BAXTER I remember when that scene came in.
Because the two of us work at the same time,
every time a day was shot, the next morning
someone was ready to grab it, which is terrific.
You really stay up to camera when there are two

people assembling. I was working on the
Caribbean Night party scene, and so when the
opening scene came in, Angus was like, "I got it."
It seemed like just another day's worth of material
arriving, but when that scene landed on Angus, it
mushroomed into a month, or a couple of weeks.

WALL I think I spent two days just piecing it
together, getting all the words strung out, and
then there was a concentrated effort over three
weeks to fine-cut it. There were three setups and
two cameras on each setup, and probably 60
run-throughs of the scene, which lasts just over
six minutes. I broke it down into five sections,
because if I had tackled the whole thing, my
head probably would have exploded. I treated
each fifth as its own scene and built each one,

"You can easily get seduced by tears," Baxter says, which is why he ended up using the least emotional take of Andrew Garfield's performance in the big falling-out scene between Eduardo and Mark. "It was a difficult decision," Wall says. "But in a film like that, if you have one huge peak, relatively speaking, it diminishes everything else."

then strung them together, saw how much it sucked, and then just continually refined and tightened it.

When you watch take after take of David's material, it's not immediately obvious what the best stuff is. He's not like Billy Wilder, who was famous for shooting a funny take of something, then a straight take of something and then a slightly sad take of something. David's always moving in a certain direction, and the spectrum he's moving in is very narrow. He's very specific about what he wants. You only start to realize this when you really break the dailies down and start comparing the line readings. I think you have to ratchet up your bullshit detector when you're watching dailies. You have to be able to say, "I'm not buying that performance," or "Maybe I buy that performance, but I'm going to look for something better." You have to be hyper-critical of everything you're watching.

BAXTER You can easily get seduced by tears in dailies, because they're hard to produce. And admittedly, it's very fine acting. I remember there was a point early on when Angus and I were concerned that Eduardo Saverin was coming off as a wimp or a wet blanket in the boardroom. And if he did, no one was going to like him.

WALL There's a scene where Eduardo says to Mark, "I was your only friend." In dailies, on a meter, Andrew Garfield was at nine-and-a-half. He had tears in his eyes, and was an emotional wreck, because it seemed like an emotional →

THE SOCIAL NETWORK

The Henley boat race was one of only two sequences in **The Social Network** (the other being the opening credits) not crammed with wall-to-wall dialogue, and thus served as a brief respite for the audience. It was also the very last scene Fincher and his crew filmed, as they had to wait until July to shoot the crowds at the Henley Royal Regatta; those were then juxtaposed with closeups of the rowers, including Tyler and Cameron Winklevoss (played by Armie Hammer), which were shot not on the Thames, but on a man-made lake in Eton. The backgrounds were digitally blurred, giving the sequence the look of tilt-shift photography, so as to focus the eye on a specific part of the frame. For Baxter and Wall, the propulsive rhythm of the scene was set by the increasingly frenzied music track composed by Trent Reznor and Atticus Ross. "We were hanging our hat on the track," Wall says. "It's like a proper music video, in a way. After doing all these intense, Swiss-engineered dialogue scenes, it was nice to do something that was a little freer."

peak in the script. But I think that bedeviled us in the cutting, and Kirk ended up using the least histrionic performance. It was a difficult decision because when we were cutting the scene, we were seduced by his performance. But in a film like that, if you have one huge peak, relatively speaking, it diminishes everything else.

BAXTER That line Eduardo has, "My father won't even look at me"—I buried that in the coverage. We had these big closeups of Andrew, too, but I did it all over-the-shoulder.

WALL There are times when you have to reconsider a whole character and ask, is that the right throughline for that character? I remember on **Panic Room** (2002), David wanted to look at all of Forest Whitaker's scenes strung together, just to make sure his character arc was doing what it was supposed to do.

Another challenge on **The Social Network** was the fact that it had a 160-page script. There was a clear desire to have it be under two hours. David actually asked Aaron Sorkin to read him

the script, and it came in at just under two hours, though I didn't know that until after the movie was done. So we ended up cutting very tight in assembly, and in fact, the first assembly of **The Social Network** was shorter than the final by two minutes. David hadn't shot the Henley boat-race scene yet.

BAXTER We had dialogue playing underneath every moment. The moment nothing was happening, even in the assembly stage, it was like a siren going off: "Dead spot! Dead spot!" The errors started to stand out by themselves.

WALL In the end, there were actually places where we had to add time, because some moments were just getting run roughshod over. We needed to add nine or ten frames to something so the audience could take a micro-breath, absorb what had just happened, and move on.

BAXTER In a movie that's moving at a machine-gun pace, ten frames is a nice pause.

WALL The great thing about what we do is that every day is different. In a way, every day you go down the rabbit hole. It's not color-by-numbers. It's more like you get a series of words and you have to put together the *New York Times* crossword puzzle. You have to figure out how everything goes together, which is hard...and fun.

BAXTER I don't know if this is because it was the first movie I was ever involved in, but even now, after having done three movies with David since, **Zodiac** still seems like the hardest one yet. And I think, editorially, it was Angus' finest hour, not only because the scenes were seamlessly done, but because the narrative of the film wasn't a given. It had to be discovered and found.

WALL I disagree. I don't think it's actually my best work because I feel I've learned a lot since then. But it is one of my favorite films because of how rewarding it was to see it come to life. It was really hard.

BAXTER Super-hard. I remember it just crushing me.

WALL I was terrified on that job, more terrified than I've ever been on any project. The challenge with the story was to keep it interesting. Basically, all the action happens in the first 30 minutes, and then there's this long procedural, and then there's an exciting scene toward the end, and then there's no "satisfying" finale, in the conventional sense. It was all about the accumulation of detail. We tried to hew as close to the truth as possible and imbue the film with as much drama as possible. There was a lot of data represented in the movie, and one of the biggest challenges was figuring out what to take out. A couple of scenes were excised, but David stuck to his guns with a lot of it. It was important to make sure that the film stayed true to the story.

BAXTER It was also challenging to make sense of all those dead ends. You go chasing after something, and then you have to stop, reverse →

"In a movie that's moving at a machine-gun pace, ten frames is a nice pause."

and back out. And when you're assembling, when everything isn't still singing perfectly, it's really easy to start picking on everything and thinking this or that should be cut out. But even if, after the first assembly, we have an idea of what scenes could go, nothing is going to be illuminated with David until it's been fine-cut to the nth degree. And in the process of fine-cutting, you end up not wanting to lose the scene.

I remember toward the end of **The Curious Case of Benjamin Button** (2008), there was a sort of mandate from David to bring down the running time. I was sort of naïve about the process in the beginning. I remember spending two days on it and saying, "Here, come have a look!" And I showed him how I had taken a few frames out of this and a little bit out of that. And he just looked at me and said, "Kirk, get to work." So I opened up a few scenes with him, and we started to eliminate the front ends, and pretty soon I said, "Oh, OK. Now I get it." We were very diligent in trying to compress the film to the best of our abilities without losing any key story or character.

WALL Everything has to get its due before you kill it. It's the proper way to work.

BAXTER I remember Angus once saying to me that he always looks for the hardest way to do things. If you do the easiest one, you might as well get someone else to do it.

WALL Did I say that? Stupid, stupid me.

BAXTER We do a lot of extra work, but I enjoy doing it. I think we're supposed to do it this way.

WALL You have to realize that there are hundreds of years of man-hours that have gone into everything that hits the screen in the edit bay. You cannot casually make decisions. You can't be cavalier about how you proceed. You may think that something's not worth being in the film, but there's a reason that it was written, performed and photographed. Everything ultimately has to be given its due. This thought is a great motivator because you feel you have to go through everything with a fine-toothed comb. And you need the time to assess what you're doing, for better or for

THE CURIOUS CASE OF BENJAMIN BUTTON

The centerpiece of this film is a tightly cut sequence detailing a daisy-chain of coincidences, missed appointments and chance encounters, culminating in the car accident that costs Daisy (Cate Blanchett) her dancing career. Baxter originally cut the sequence at a more languid pace before overlaying Brad Pitt's voiceover and Alexandre Desplat's music, which imposed a quicker rhythm and required him to compress the sequence by reducing the number of frames in each shot. The result, a taut meditation-in-miniature on the irreversibility of time and the inevitability of fate, "was one of the easiest scenes to edit, because it was kind of like action," Baxter recalls. "It was a lot of fun."

worse. That's where the enjoyment of the job actually comes from, is spending the time.

BAXTER It helps that we are so fast and efficient now. There was a lot more time-wasting back in the old days. I was trained as an assistant on film, so I started off with Steenbecks and cutting with rolls. All the dailies would come in, and my editor would mark his favorite takes, and I would hang the takes on a trim bin and assemble the roll in the order I thought he would cut it in. I was like the monkey on his shoulder, ready to grab whatever he needed.

WALL I cut film once, I think when I was eight or nine. It was a stop-motion Super 8 film that I made with a G.I. Joe. I made other films after that, but I shot them so I would never have to edit them because I was so bad at physically cutting the film. I think I made two splices and my mom helped me to do the rest. I learned how to edit on linear videotape, which taught me to commit. You had to get it right, or had to dub the tape to another tape, lose a generation and then what you were showing people was going to look like crap. One of the cool things about post-production is that it's always in a state of flux, especially since digital entered the equation. I switched over from Avid to Final Cut Pro six years ago, and we're always on the lookout for something better.

Every tool has its idiosyncrasies. You can be insanely inefficient with these tools, or you can be insanely efficient with them. The fewer links you have in the chain going from photographer to editor, the better. There are fewer opportunities for things to go wrong, and there's more accountability on every link. We definitely have it down to a minimum.

BAXTER Yeah, we have it humming away now. I do remember about three weeks ago, David asked me if I had taken a look at a scene from **The Girl with the Dragon Tattoo** that he'd just shot the day before. I said I hadn't gotten to it yet, and he made some comment to the effect of, "We've got

to speed this up." But it's so fast already. He can get it to the point where it leaps out of his camera and straight into my lap, but I still can't cut it as fast as he's filming it.

WALL But that's good, because the logjam, then, is the creative part. We're not spending our time waiting for stuff to get transcoded. We're the thing that's taking the time, which is how it should be.

BAXTER I've always had help from the moment we stepped into the world of Avid and Final Cut. It's constantly changing so much, I don't put a lot of energy into thinking about it. I just concentrate on what's in the frame, and I'm able to be that way because I work with Angus.

WALL Cutting movies can be such a lonely endeavor. Why not have a partner? I know when we're on the movie together, it's a lot more fun than when we're working individually. There's somebody there to share the burden, the pressure and the responsibility. And because we work together, there are times when one of us can go off and do a commercial and then come back to the film. We're incredibly fortunate to be able to do that. It's kind of ideal.

BAXTER It's really helpful to have these two careers running, and you really have to take care of both. You can't ignore one, because it will ignore you if you do. The fact that we can sink into commercials from time to time means we don't have to take certain movies on. We don't have to do the movie about huskies.

WALL That was a good movie.

Lee Smith

"I still make it a point to think hard about what I'm doing, so as not to forget my training as a film editor. I know I can fiddle, but my rule remains: Do it once right."

Born in 1960 in Sydney, Lee Smith had plenty of encouragement to enter the film business while he was growing up, considering his father worked as an optical effects supervisor and his uncle owned a film-processing lab. After learning multiple film disciplines at a local post-production company, during which he edited a number of science-fiction thrillers including **Communion** (1989) and **RoboCop 2** (1990), and served as an assistant editor, additional editor and sound designer on such Peter Weir dramas as **The Year of Living Dangerously** (1982), **Dead Poets Society** (1989), **Green Card** (1990) and **Fearless** (1993), Smith was hired to co-edit Weir's **The Truman Show** (1998) with William M. Anderson. He has since received solo editing credits on the Australian director's **Master and Commander: The Far Side of the World** (2003) and **The Way Back** (2010).

Smith has also enjoyed a collaboration with Christopher Nolan, for whom he edited **Batman Begins** (2005), **The Prestige** (2006), **The Dark Knight** (2008) and **Inception** (2010). He received two Academy Award and ACE Eddie nominations for his work on **Master and Commander** and **The Dark Knight**. His other credits include Gregor Jordan's **Buffalo Soldiers** (2001), Craig Lahiff's **Black and White** (2002), and Matthew Vaughn's upcoming **X-Men: First Class** (2011).

Lee Smith

" I started cutting on a Moviola, which is that clackety-clack thing you see in old movies. I eventually graduated to a Steenbeck and a KEM, those big flatbed editing machines, which I worked on for years. My first non-linear editing experience was on Lightworks. There was a lot about that I loved, but I hated the image quality, which was so poor that I couldn't believe it was ever going to take off. But that changed very rapidly, and now I'm using an Avid, as I have for at least ten years. You can't go back; it's just not possible.

Still, I would've hated to miss cutting on film. Running the reels backward and forward gives you time to think. And I still make it a point to think hard about what I'm doing, so as not to forget my training as a film editor. I know I can fiddle, but my rule remains: Do it once right.

Non-linear or non-destructive editing is fantastic because you get to play. You get to change things and keep things, which you couldn't do on film. You couldn't just sit there and fiddle, because the mechanical method of cutting was mostly about keeping the work print in good condition, and it would take so much time to make a single splice. I cut so many movies that way and never thought twice about it. Nowadays, I watch editors who haven't had film experience, and they tend to jump around a lot, as if they've all got ADD. They can't calm down and just look at something. Because it's non-linear, that's the way their brains work now.

Films look better when they're shot on film. The film process is still superior to the digital process, which makes me wonder why everyone's racing to convert to something that is still theoretically catching up. It's a weird thing. In digital, it's always "almost as good as film." If it's almost as good, my suggestion is to keep it in your back pocket and then bring it out again when it's better—which will happen, of course.

I got my start as an apprentice at a small post-production company. This was during the early days of the Australian film industry, and people like Peter Weir, Phillip Noyce, Gillian Armstrong, and Jane Campion were coming up through those facilities, though none of them was well known yet. I worked my way up, learning how to operate sound equipment and fix editing

THE TRUMAN SHOW

This film proved difficult to edit, not least because it was unclear exactly how explicit the film should be about its central premise. Initially, it became quite obvious early on that Truman Burbank (Jim Carrey) was the unwitting subject of his own TV show, due to numerous scenes of supporting characters smiling directly at the camera. At director Peter Weir's request, Smith ended up cutting a brand-new prologue that introduced the characters yet remained cagey about the true nature of their role in Truman's life.

All in all, the film (which was co-edited by William M. Anderson) was screened in about 18 different versions before Weir and Smith settled on their final cut. Finding the right structure required a delicate balancing act. "Sometimes it got better and better, and other times it just crashed and burned," Smith says. "There were a couple of screenings where you'd be forgiven for asking, 'Wow, is that the same movie?'"

machines and project films; you had to be a real jack of all trades. I was offered the opportunity to do the sound on a couple of very B-grade movies no one else wanted to work on. And eventually I managed to get onto **The Year of Living Dangerously** (1982), which was my entry into quality filmmaking and the first time I met Peter Weir.

The way Peter shoots is very organic; he covers scenes in many varied ways, as he demonstrated on **The Truman Show** (1998). We originally planned to start that film by essentially letting the audience in on the it's-all-a-TV-show gag, right at the beginning. We had many shots of characters looking down the barrel of the lens with a wry smile. Very quickly we realized this wasn't the right tactic. Peter told me he wasn't happy with the beginning of the film and asked me to come up with something different. Fortunately, we had a **Truman Show** mockumentary that had been filmed, and from that I managed to find all the material with which to assemble the actual prologue of the film. So it was just a matter of working my way through the footage. Peter tends to shoot more than he needs.

It was a very complicated film to edit. Peter would push the envelope by having us change even parts of the film that were working and move them around, just in the hunt for the best possible result. Sometimes it got better and better, and other times it just crashed and burned. We did about 18 screenings of that film, and there were a couple of screenings where you'd be forgiven for asking, "Wow, is that the same movie?"

Every film is like a puzzle, and you just have to keep watching it, and eventually you can tell where the stumbling blocks are. Then it's just a matter of repositioning them, and the effect of that can change the entire outcome of the movie. Simply moving and manipulating sequences can derail a film. You can build a film for either complete destruction or complete success in the editing room, and I've definitely seen both. But you have to watch the whole movie to be able to tell, and I think a lot of editors make mistakes because they don't take that step. How many movies have you seen where you watch a 20-minute chunk and you think it's genius, →

MASTER AND COMMANDER: THE FAR SIDE OF THE WORLD

The sequence in which Dr. Stephen Maturin (Paul Bettany) performs a brave feat of auto-surgery represents an especially deft example of how restrained editing can yield both humor and tension in the same moment. Smith cut from Capt. Jack Aubrey (Russell Crowe) and other quietly horrified onlookers to tight close-ups of Maturin's clenched face, never showing the wound itself in detail, but rather leaving the audience members to imagine the pain on their own.

and then another 10-minute chunk that's not so genius? You drop in and out of the film, and every so often it's amazing, but when you watch it as a whole, it does not work. You, the editor, have got to make the movie work as a whole; that's how they're designed to run. The more you can keep watching the movie, the more it'll throw its issues back in your face.

Master and Commander: The Far Side of the World (2003) was the first film Peter asked me to cut as sole editor, and it was the first time I'd worked with that kind of budget. I loved everything about that movie, though we had a rocky ride in post. Neither Peter nor I had worked on big, effects-heavy films, and there were so many holes and placeholders, which was a bit awkward. When you're not used to it, the footage just looks disgusting with all the greenscreen and cranes and crap in the shots. You're sitting there, wondering, "Is this ever going to look good?" The first assembly was four hours long; it was a big, unwieldy beast of a movie. The terrific thing about Peter is that he's really good at removing what needs to be removed. It might have been the hardest sequence in the world to shoot, and he could look at it once and say, "Take it out. It's not for the movie."

A good example of that was on **Dead Poets Society** (1989). I had cut a very funny scene in which Robin Williams' character is teaching the boys the art of concentration. He's got an overhead projector and the boys are all taking an exam, and he tells them, "Eyes down, eyes down." And then he starts putting nudes on the projector. It was funny as hell, and we were all sitting there killing ourselves laughing. Peter laughed and laughed like he's never laughed before. And as soon as the scene was finished, he said, "Take it out. It's a great scene, but that's not the character." And when I reflect upon it, I believe he was 100 percent right: That was not the character. As good as that scene was, it didn't belong in the movie. Over the years I've learned to be able to look objectively at something and say, "Brilliant scene, but it does nothing, and it's got to go." →

Stages of cutting

Editor's cut: "Post-production" can be a misleading term, as as the editor starts working at the same time principal photography begins. In cutting scenes together from dailies and placing them in the structure dictated by the script, the editor will make every effort to stay "up to camera," so that the initial assembly will be complete shortly after shooting ends. Because it essentially represents a rough draft, the editor's cut is often longer than the film will end up being.

Director's cut: Once shooting has wrapped, the director will join the editor in the cutting room and the two will work together to improve and refine the cut of the film. Reshoots may be conducted during this period if needed. Directors Guild of America rules stipulate that directors have a minimum of ten weeks after completion of principal photography to prepare their cut.

Final cut: The final cut of the film is determined and supervised by the film's producer(s), although in some cases the director may negotiate with the studio to receive final cut approval.

"Generally speaking, I only read a script once—unless it's a Chris Nolan film, in which case I read it about five times."

I'm continually surprised when I cut scenes and look at them and think, well, that kind of works, but I don't quite remember how I got there. You just have to trust your gut and your intuition. I don't question what I think the first time around. As Chris Nolan says, there are a million ways to cut a scene, but only one correct one. When you look at a mountain of material, if you start questioning your own thoughts, you'll just turn into a puddle and it will take you three years to edit the movie.

Generally speaking, I only read a script once—unless it's a Chris Nolan film, in which case I read it about five times. **Inception** (2010) was probably the most intense editorial experience of my life. I was finishing Peter Weir's **The Way Back** (2010) when production on **Inception** began, so I had my assistant, John Lee, do the initial assembly for Chris. I came on quite late, and we were probably within a couple of months of finishing shooting, and Chris didn't want me to look at any of the work John had done. He wanted me to assemble strictly from dailies, which I was somewhat anticipating. The advantage was that I was able to come in while the film was still being shot and start from scene one, which I've never been able to do in my life, though I'm not sure whether that ended up making the film make any more sense to me. There was a huge amount of coverage and an enormous number of conceptual ideas being bounced around while they were shooting. The script, of course, is helpful at first. But once the film is shot, the script becomes irrelevant, and you have to cut with what you're given. Let the images do the talking.

The cross-cutting among dream levels was especially challenging. My approach, as with all editing, was to construct each sequence as a standalone, and then I would start to intercut, and

intercut, and intercut, working out where all the best transition points were. Some of those were script-based, some weren't, and some I just discovered as I proceeded. It was like a gigantic game of chess, and I would just have to keep making my moves. Occasionally I would make the wrong move, and I'd realize that a certain sequence had gone on too long and I had lost the thread. But truthfully, there were so many ticking clocks, it would actually become quite obvious when I had it wrong, because I would cut back to something and realize it didn't work.

In editing, as in mathematics and music, we all have an in-built clock. When your clock is off kilter or out of step, you tend to feel it quite strongly. I certainly do. It's like a sledgehammer. If I watch something and it's wrong, it's not subtly wrong. It's like an alarm bell that goes off. The trick is to keep screening the film and get it to the point where you know it feels right. →

THE DARK KNIGHT

Heath Ledger's performance as the Joker in **The Dark Knight** underscored the intense physicality of the film, particularly in the editing, as Smith used sharp, jolting cuts so that the punches and blows would register with particularly visceral force. Still, he and Nolan opted to limit Ledger's exposure, knowing that his performance, strong as it was, would be more effective in small, potent doses. "It was the old adage of 'Keep them wanting more,'" says Smith, who had previously edited Ledger's work in the Australian film **Two Hands** (1999).

THE PRESTIGE

Despite the strength of the script, the first cut of **The Prestige** was surprisingly clunky, according to Smith. "Neither Chris Nolan nor I cared for it much the first time," he says. "But then it became really good, really fast. Within a couple of weeks, we managed to crack it."

Their method in assembling the film, with its brisk shifts back and forth in time, was to make the puzzle bulletproof, so that there would be a satisfactory answer to any question a viewer could pose. This required maintaining certain key lines of dialogue in the film despite the usual pressure to trim it down. "Chris would always say, 'No. If we take that out, we're cheating.'"

The first time we screened **Inception** was probably about four weeks or so into Chris' director's cut. There were just four of us: Chris; Emma, his wife; John Lee, my additional editor/ assistant; and myself. I felt pretty reasonable about it, but it was such a complicated film that I was nonetheless on the edge of my seat, wondering if we had cracked all the nuts that needed to be cracked. That first screening was amazing. The film worked so well. We were all sort of sitting there with our mouths hanging open. I had thought it would be the mother of all problems—the Rubix cube of filmmaking.

Of course, if you thought **Inception** was complicated, **The Prestige** (2006) was even more so. When you're editing a puzzle movie, the rule is: Don't cheat. When you establish a mechanism or a condition of the film's world, don't cheat. In film, you can cheat endlessly; it's the lazy way of doing it. You think no one will notice, but it always ends up letting the audience down. We wanted to make **The Prestige** bulletproof, so that at the end of the day, people could question it to death and there would always be an answer to every question. It can be dangerous when you're trimming down; some lines of dialogue are essential parts of the film's DNA. Some of them perhaps seemed not so useful, the type you could get away with trimming, but Chris would always say, "No. If we take that out, we're cheating."

I never want to mystify or confuse an audience without good reason. There are moments in any film when you can use confusion well, but I never want someone to come up to me after that film and say, "What was that?" or "I didn't understand it at all." Of course there's a small percentage of people who will fall into that category. But a film's success is evidence that the film did indeed translate to a reasonably broad audience, which gives me faith that "reasonably broad" means "reasonably smart." You respect the audience, and it works. **"**

INCEPTION
Cutting among the various dream levels in **Inception** "was like a gigantic game of chess," says Smith. "I would just have to keep making my moves." He constructed each level in standalone sequences before intercutting the individual strands; at one point, the film is so fiendishly complex that four different parallel levels are in play. Still, Smith notes, "There were so many ticking clocks, it would actually become quite obvious when I had it wrong."

Christopher Rouse

"In the end, if you like our style, great. If you don't, to each his own. Since the beginning films have spoken to us in many different styles. As for me, I enjoy them all."

A third-generation filmmaker, Christopher Rouse first learned how to edit while working for his father, the writer, director and producer Russell Rouse. After serving as an apprentice and assistant editor on various film and television productions in the 1980s, he received his first feature-editing credit on Michael Cimino's **Desperate Hours** (1990). He spent the next eleven years primarily editing for television, including the miniseries **From the Earth to the Moon** (1998) and **Anne Frank: The Whole Story** (2001), before working as additional editor on Doug Liman's **The Bourne Identity** (2002).

Paul Greengrass directed the next two installments of the Matt Damon-starring franchise, launching a collaboration with Rouse that includes not only **The Bourne Supremacy** (2003, with Richard Pearson) and **The Bourne Ultimatum** (2007), but also **United 93** (2006, with Pearson and Clare Douglas) and **Green Zone** (2010). **The Bourne Ultimatum** won Rouse the Academy Award, the ACE Eddie Award and the BAFTA for best editing, while he, Pearson and Douglas were also Oscar-nominated for their work on **United 93**. Rouse's other editing credits include F. Gary Gray's **The Italian Job** (2003, with Richard Francis-Bruce), John Woo's **Paycheck** (2003) and Frank Marshall's **Eight Below** (2006).

Christopher Rouse

" Even when I was making my own Super 8 films as a kid, editing was the part of the process I enjoyed the most. As much as I love working with actors and shooting footage, editing was where I felt the film came together, and I was always compelled by the process of writing with the film and putting the final stamp on it. My first job out of high school was on one of my father's films, and while my father supported my dream of working in motion pictures, he was reticent to encourage my career in such an uncertain field. He said that while he would help me find a way in, what I did after that was up to me. I headed straight for the cutting room and spent as much time as I could there, and I was lucky enough to have a wonderful editor named Bud Isaacs who took me under his wing. From the moment I stepped into the cutting room with Bud, I knew I was home.

I came onto **The Italian Job** halfway through the project, and one of the issues the piece had was that it sagged a bit in the second act. As I was looking through some discarded third-act material, I stumbled upon footage shot by a second unit director who had been replaced.

It had been intended for the third-act car chase and was now obsolete, but there were some good moments in it. I decided to repurpose the material, putting it into the second act as part of a new "dry run" montage, with the characters testing their Mini Coopers. That's an example of something I love about editing. I enjoy the challenge of seeing what some of the difficulties may have been with a piece and coming up with solutions, whether it's in shooting additional material or cannibalizing existing footage. One of the great rewards of our process is in finding the full potential of the film—sometimes as it was originally intended, and sometimes in an entirely reimagined way.

Indeed, one of the great blessings of working with Paul Greengrass is that he is constantly thinking out of the box, and isn't necessarily married to what's on the page. For example, if we're talking about dailies and I tell him, honestly, I don't think there's a snowball's chance in hell that we're going to need the back end of a particular scene, he'll say, "Well, leave it out of the cut." The script isn't the Bible for us. That has nothing to do with the quality of the writing;

THE BOURNE ULTIMATUM

Much of the Tangiers sequence in **The Bourne Ultimatum** was underscored by a music cue that composer John Powell had originally written for **The Bourne Supremacy**. Yet Rouse and Greengrass agreed that the music should end the moment Bourne leapt off the balcony railing and through the window to confront Desh (Joey Ansah), the assassin tailing Nicky Parsons (Julia Stiles). "Paul and I absolutely didn't want to hear music during the fight," Rouse says, noting that the hand-to-hand combat between Bourne and Desh "would feel much more raw and visceral played dry."

we've worked with some brilliant writers who have generated fantastic work. But Paul's background is in documentaries, and on set he responds to the organic flow of a scene as it develops—often revising as he goes. And similarly, as our film evolves in the cutting room, we are constantly in search of the "truth" of the piece—even if it takes us away from what was originally written.

Most editors try to adapt their styles to suit the piece in question. On the **Bourne** movies, the style was born, no pun intended, out of what the material inherently dictated. Paul shoots in a very kind of caught, verité style; it's all about the immediacy of the moment. There's an incredible vibrancy to his footage.

His dailies are not like dailies I've experienced from any other director. In a given setup, a shot might start in a certain place, and the camera might move to another place and then to another, and so on. Take two may be generally the same, but have some distinct variations; there may be moments caught that weren't found the first time. As opposed to dealing with more staid, predictable footage where changes in performance may be →

Bourne to be a winner

Winning an Academy Award is, as they say, the thrill of a lifetime. Rouse, who was nominated for **United 93** and won the following year for **The Bourne Ultimatum**, recounts his very different back-to-back experiences attending the Oscars.

Distant hopes: "A friend of mine said to me, 'Where they seat you will probably give you a pretty good indication of your chances of winning. For **United 93**, Paul [Greengrass] and I were literally by the door on the right-hand side of the theater. We were practically sitting next to the toilet. I turned and looked at Paul and said, 'Well, I think I can relax tonight.'"

In the hot seat: "The next year, I was lucky enough to win the BAFTA and the Eddie Award for **The Bourne Ultimatum**, so I thought, 'Wow, maybe I actually have a shot at the Oscar,' even though I truly thought the Coen brothers were going to run the table with **No Country for Old Men**. At the Oscars, as soon as I sat down, a woman came up to me and said, 'OK, Mr. Rouse, now your category's going to be two-thirds of the way through the show, and it's really important that you don't get up before the commercial break.' Immediately I felt myself begin to sweat profusely inside my tuxedo."

Winning in retrospect: "I don't say this out of any sense of false modesty, and I love the fact that I won an award, but I think editing is just so difficult to judge. Unlike something where what you see is what you get, whether it's a score, cinematography or production design, you don't really know what an editor's been given to work with. Personally, I think it's easier to pull nuance out of really great material than it is to take something that's fundamentally broken and make it fairly watchable. That may be the bigger feat, but it's something nobody will ever recognize."

the only variable, in editing Paul's material you have to be aware of other variations as well.

When I'm cutting films with other directors, I usually build scenes in a more conventional way, pulling from the original daily clips. With Paul's material, because the camerawork is so free-form, I'll break down the shots into "like" components before I begin cutting. In other words, I might lump together the pieces of one character in a single clip—containing all that character's dialogue and reactions, and then another's, and so forth. Other sequences may have different times of cutaways or interesting moments I think belong in the film. It becomes a much more labor-intensive process, but practically, it allows me to access the material in a much more functional way, and to fully inhabit the scene before I make a proper cut. By the time I'm ready to edit, I have a pretty clear sense of what the architecture of the scene should be.

This process reminds me of what I appreciated about cutting on film—especially flatbeds. To get to a piece of film that was 500 feet into a roll on KEM, you often had to wind through those 500 feet, sometimes seeing pieces along the way that would ignite an idea. The great blessing of systems like Avid is that you can get material immediately, but as a result, you may not watch takes straight through as many times as you would on a linear system. Not that I'd ever want to go back; if I had to cut Paul's movies on film, I'd probably still be cutting them.

If I've done my homework—immersing myself in the story, characters and the director's vision—my cutting is more intuitive than cognitive. Obviously many of the issues an editor deals with must be thought through logically, but I know I'm in a good place when I'm just reacting to and interacting with what's in front of me. Because Paul gives me more freedom than any other director I've worked with, he says our relationship is a little bit like playing jazz, which I think is pretty accurate. There's something so liberating about his footage; even on a carefully planned scene like the Waterloo sequence in **The Bourne Ultimatum**, there were many different ways to put it together in the cutting room, but because Paul and I were very much on the same page, my early pass at that sequence was not far afield from where we wound up.

One of the many things Paul does exceedingly well is get everybody on his crew to engage with his ideas. Paul defines dramatic stakes very well, so that as you track your way through a narrative, you're aware of not only what's important plot-wise, but also the thematic issues and subtexts supporting characters' evolutions. The hand-to-hand fight in Tangiers in **The Bourne Ultimatum** is not just about the hero going to save the girl; it's about an assassin who inherently doesn't want to kill but has to. In terms of the mechanics of that scene, Paul and I absolutely didn't want to hear music during the fight, just as we didn't want music for a similar fight scene in **The Bourne Supremacy**. We felt both scenes would feel much more raw and visceral played dry, particularly the Tangiers fight since it occurs after a 20-minute music cue. The music ends when Bourne jumps through the window, and the sudden absence of the cue makes the fight seem much more real.

I remember watching dailies of the hand-to-hand fights in **Supremacy** and **Ultimatum** and seeing images that were very obscure, where I wasn't entirely sure what I was looking at, realizing that if I cut too quickly I ran the risk of losing the audience. It is a bit of a high-wire act; we do sacrifice a bit of geography in the Bourne films, but the tradeoff is that the style becomes much more subjective, which is fitting, because if you've ever been in a fight, it's a very chaotic, violent occurrence where you don't have your bearings. We pursued a similar strategy with the car chases: Paul and his second unit director, Dan Bradley, brilliantly placed the camera in such a way that the audience is right there with Bourne as he's being slammed around.

Paul always wants to know how I'm reacting to the material that he's sending me, and while he's shooting we will generally speak a couple of times every day. Early on, when I was cutting the opening Berlin sequence in **Ultimatum** when →

THE BOURNE ULTIMATUM

The Waterloo station chase in **The Bourne Ultimatum**
offers a prime example of the quicksilver cross-cutting
techniques deployed by Rouse and director Paul
Greengrass. Darting from Jason Bourne (Matt Damon) to
marked man Simon Ross (Paddy Considine) to the other
characters attempting to monitor their activity amid the
bustle of early-morning commuters, the camera seems
to be everywhere at once, yet always feeds the viewer
enough information to maintain a visually and narratively
coherent throughline.

UNITED 93

One of the most powerful and deliberate juxtapositions in **United 93** was the repeated cross-cutting between hijacker Ahmed Al Haznawi (Omar Berdouni) assembling the bomb in the airplane bathroom and passengers receiving their meal service. "It's an incredible contrast of events," Rouse says. "On one hand you see people engaged in the most mundane behavior, and on the other you see a man preparing to change the course of our world. Those were our last moments of being normal, before our lives were turned completely upside down."

Bourne is going through the train yard, I felt the original staging of it wasn't working as well as it should, so Paul and I discussed what to do about it. While we were trying to figure out the most effective way to enter and button the scene, at a certain point I said, "Every time I'm dealing with a scene in this film, it just feels like I want to put my foot to the floor, pace-wise, and not let up." Paul agreed, and so we decided to just do it and see what happened. We were both looking to strengthen the engine of **Ultimatum**. By the third installment of the **Bourne** series, we didn't have a story driver quite as strong as those on the first and second films—the sense of discovery in **Identity**, the revenge and redemption motives in **Supremacy**. Paul and I both felt we needed to create a style for the piece that was evocative of Bourne's urgent need to discover who he was, and there had to be a breathless quality about it.

I was fortunate to cut **Supremacy** with a very good friend of mine, Rick Pearson, who's a superb editor. We'd bat ideas back and forth all the time, and I think we're both better editors for having worked together. The best co-editing situations occur when people check their egos at the door and are open to each other's ideas. I've never understood people who believe they have all the answers creatively. Anybody working in this collaborative art form who thinks they're right all the time is simply wrong. I want to hear different ideas and different points of view, because I think it challenges me and ultimately makes → the film better. Rick and I work together seamlessly. That came in especially handy on **United 93**, which is to date the toughest picture I've ever done, because of the nature of the material and the tightness of our deadline. I never would have made it without Rick. For example, the cockpit-charge sequence was all him; he did a brilliant job with it.

Paul filmed **United 93** in a way that he hadn't shot anything before with me. He kept the cameras rolling continuously, so that the B camera would reload while the A camera was shooting. It was an ingenious technique—Paul kept going and going, and the actors were getting fractured and frayed, which in the end got them to a profoundly truthful place during those scenes. Paul often shot eight tracks of overlapping, improvised dialogue; I had to hire a team of assistants just to mark every single line of dialogue so they could be located. And because it was like cutting a documentary, it became a very, very labor-intensive process. There was also the emotional content of the material. I'm always emotionally engaged in the pieces that I work with; in 2001 I cut a miniseries called **Anne Frank: The Whole Story**, and I was deeply affected by that. One of the last scenes I worked on in United 93 was the scene with the passengers making phone calls home. I remember it was two or three in the morning, and I had to stop because I had broken down crying. And it wasn't the first time.

Paul did a tremendous amount of research on **United 93**. He didn't want to make a polemic; he wanted to deliver a document that he felt was a reasonably accurate snapshot of that day. To that end, he created an environment on set where people could just be. It was quite remarkable— there were only a few moments when I could tell the actors were acting as opposed to behaving in character, and that is a great testimony to Paul's ability to deliver verisimilitude.

One of the most interesting juxtapositions in **United 93** occurs when one hijacker goes into the bathroom of the plane to begin to assemble the bomb, and it's intercut with people having their meal service. It's an incredible contrast of events—on one hand you see people engaged in the most mundane behavior, and on the other you see a man preparing to change the course of our world. As we cut from the hijacker to a passenger eating his or her last meal, we begin to understand that those were our last moments of being normal, before our lives were turned completely upside down.

I was on **Green Zone** (2010) for two years, from beginning to end. It was a very difficult film for all of us. The studio and the filmmakers had →

EIGHT BELOW

While perhaps not the first film that comes to mind when one thinks of Rouse's style, Frank Marshall's **Eight Below** presented a unique editorial challenge in that it required Rouse to construct scenes and an overall narrative around several four-legged, non-verbal camera subjects, often by alternating between the dogs' facial expressions and point-of-view shots. "It was almost like cutting a silent film," Rouse muses. "It was great for me, too, because my kids could watch it, unlike a lot of my other films."

the best intentions as we moved forward, but we were hit hard by the writers' strike, and we had to fix a lot of things during production that we wouldn't have had to otherwise. Of the four films I've done with Paul, I'd say **Green Zone** was the toughest one to bring to the finish line, but I'm very proud of it. I felt that, at the end of the day, the film stood up tall and strong.

A number of sequences presented challenges, such as one where the Americans attack the Iraqi safehouse where Matt Damon's character (Roy Miller) is being held. There were several storylines that had to be tracked clearly and simultaneously: Miller being caught and interrogated, two special-forces groups converging on the house, Iraqi insurgents preparing for battle, CIA and DOD characters trying to understand what was occurring, and Miller's translator ostensibly coming to his aid. Another challenging sequence was when Miller's team invaded a home where Iraqi generals were meeting. I ended up making significant changes to the staging of that scene, which originally had Miller and his team arriving and then watching most of the generals leave. I said to Paul, "I'm not sure why they're waiting. They're there, why don't they act?" So I intercut the generals leaving with Miller's drive to the house, which not only made more sense, but was more dramatic since the scene now had "a clock" on it.

Paul's nature is probative. He wants to examine the human condition, in the collective and the specific, and so in **Green Zone**, he was →

particularly well suited to the challenge of taking the film's thematic issues—how politics create our national identity, how individuals grapple with issues of right and wrong in a morally ambiguous time, and so forth. His style allows the audience to engage with these issues in a more visceral, evocative way than a more staid piece might.

Paul and I are very open and honest with each other, and we joke constantly. If he's had a tough day on set he might say something like "I sent you a dog's dinner of rushes today," and I'll say, "Well, wait 'til I get done with them because they won't be watchable in any form." We're both reasonably self-deprecating, and we both work very, very hard. It's a serious business making multimillion-dollar films and the subject matter that Paul engages with is generally quite serious, but neither one of us takes ourselves too seriously.

There are people who dislike our style, and that's totally understandable. For my part, I was weaned on classic American filmmakers—for example, Welles, Ford, Hawks, Wilder, Capra and Sturges—and I'm a drop-dead fan of David Lean. And even though I might cut a film very aggressively, I love films that are languid and deliberate; I can still go watch an Antonioni film and just bathe in it. Like some, I do lament Western consumer culture where so much is ephemeral and our information is byte-sized. But some people conclude that's what's bad about, say, the **Bourne** films—that their style contributes to an audience with a shorter attention span. I think that's the wrong leap to make. You can point to stylistic influences that were just as aggressive 50 years ago; the easy example is **Breathless**. I believe factors such as the way our information is marketed has much more to do with the transitory nature of our culture than quick cutting in a motion picture.

In the end, if you like our style, great. If you don't, to each his own. Since the beginning films have spoken to us in many different styles. As for me, I enjoy them all.

GREEN ZONE
This film featured a number of complex set pieces, such as this one in which Rouse had to intercut among a number of simultaneous events: the capture of Capt. Roy Miller (Damon) by the forces of Iraqi Gen. Al Rawy; the goings-on at US headquarters under CIA agent Martin Brown (Brendan Gleeson); the attempted raid on Al Rawy's safehouse by two different US military factions; and the actions taken by Miller's presumed Iraqi ally, Freddy (Khalid Abdalla). "It was all about trying to keep all the balls in the air, while maintaining a sense of tension before the attack," Rouse recalls.

Universal Pictures

In an example of how an editor can affect the timing and execution of a scripted scene, Rouse opted to speed up one crucial sequence in **Green Zone**, in which Miller and his men invade a home where a number of Iraqi generals have convened. Rather than have Miller arrive and wait for the generals to file out, Rouse intercut between the two sides, so that Miller is on his way to the house while the generals are departing. Per Rouse, this "not only made more sense, but was more dramatic since the scene now had a 'clock' on it."

Sally Menke

Sally Menke's life and career were cut tragically short at the age of 56, though not before she had staked a claim to one of the most distinctive and indelible director–editor relationships in contemporary filmmaking. From **Reservoir Dogs** (1992) to **Inglourious Basterds** (2009), Menke edited every film directed by Quentin Tarantino, who often described her as his most important collaborator, and whom she helped establish a body of work unique in its structural complexity, energy and precision.

A New York native born in 1953, Menke studied film at NYU's Tisch School of the Arts and earned her earliest credits on such television documentaries as **Hans Bethe: Prophet of Energy** (1980) and **The Congress** (1988). The first feature she edited was Bruce van Dusen's 1983 romantic comedy **Cold Feet**, which was followed by the live-action **Teenage Mutant Ninja Turtles** (1990).

Menke was hiking in Canada when she received the news that Tarantino had hired her to edit his debut, **Reservoir Dogs**. With that film and its even more attention-grabbing follow-up, **Pulp Fiction** (1994), Tarantino unveiled an exciting, widely imitated cinematic style known for its intricate play with chronology, deft way with action and often startling juxtapositions of comedy and violence.

"Editors are the quiet heroes of movies," Menke said in a 2009 interview with *The New York Observer*. "And I like it that way." No doubt one of her most important contributions to Tarantino's work was her precision cutting of his lengthy, often daringly attenuated dialogue scenes, notably on display in his 1997 Elmore Leonard adaptation **Jackie Brown**. The director's next opus, a violent revenge thriller starring Uma Thurman, posed its own editorial challenges when Miramax Films chief Harvey Weinstein decided it should be cut and released as two films: **Kill Bill: Vol. 1** (2003) and **Kill Bill: Vol. 2** (2004). These were followed by **Death Proof**, Tarantino's entry in the two-part exploitation-movie throwback **Grindhouse** (2007),

01 Pulp Fiction

02 Reservoir Dogs

03 Kill Bill: Volume 1

04 Inglourious Basterds

and his World War II fantasy **Inglourious Basterds** (2009), which earned her an Academy Award nomination for best editing (she was also nominated for **Pulp Fiction**).

Menke also edited pictures for other directors, including Oliver Stone's **Heaven & Earth** (1993), Ole Bornedal's **Nightwatch** (1997), and Billy Bob Thornton's 2000 adaptation of **All the Pretty Horses** (which she also executive-produced) and **Daddy and Them** (2001). She received her final editing credit on Michael Lander's thriller **Peacock** (2010).

Menke died Sept. 27, 2010, during a hike in Griffith Park, Los Angeles, on the hottest day ever recorded in the city. She was survived by her husband, the director Dean Parisot, and their two children.

Glossary

ADR (Automatic Dialogue Replacement)
The process of replacing dialogue in post-production by an actor who repeats lines in sync with the original recording, thus ensuring a clearer dialogue track (also known as looping).

Assembly
The editor's first pass at cutting a film, consisting of selected takes joined together in script order (also known as the Rough Cut).

Avid
The trademark of a type of digital non-linear editing system.

Closeup
An image of a subject filmed at close range.

Cold cut
Cutting to a scene where there is nothing happening. To be avoided, as it stops the forward movement of the film.

Continuity editing
The predominant mode of editing in narrative cinema, predicated on maintaining coherence from shot to shot.

Coverage
The breaking up of a master shot into a variety of closer shots and angles, allowing for smooth cutting among different perspectives in a scene.

Cross-cutting
An editing technique in which the camera cuts between two or more parallel lines of action, usually to establish events occurring at the same time but in different places (also known as intercutting).

Dailies
The raw, unedited picture and sound material shot during film production (also known as rushes).

Dissolve
An editing technique that overlaps two consecutive shots, gradually transitioning from the end of one shot to the beginning of the next.

Eyeline match
A continuity editing technique in which a shot of a character looking at something offscreen is followed by a cut to the object he or she is looking at.

Fade-in
An editing technique in which a shot begins in darkness and gradually lightens to full brightness, often used at the beginning of a scene.

Fade-out
An editing technique in which a fully lit shot gradually dims to total darkness, often used at the end of a scene.

Feet
A unit of measurement for film footage; each foot of film is made up of 16 frames.

Final Cut
A non-linear editing software developed by Macromedia Inc. and later purchased by Apple Inc.

Flatbed editor
A type of film-editing device that enables picture and sound rolls to be loaded onto separate wheels and synchronized. The two most common brands of flatbed editor, the Steenbeck and the KEM (Keller-Elektro-Mechanik), were invented in Germany and became popular in the US in the 1970s.

Frame
One of many single images in a motion picture. Film is projected at 24 frames per second.

Jump cut
A cut between two shots of the same subject taken from only slightly varying angles, creating a feeling of discontinuity.

Jumping the line
When two actors are speaking to each other in a scene, they are positioned on an imaginary 180° line, which the camera must not cross. If this rule is broken, it is called jumping, or crossing the line, and proves disorienting to the viewer.

Linear editing
A method of video editing that requires the material to be assembled in an ordered sequence.

Long shot
A shot that shows an entire object or human figure from enough of a distance to place it in relation to its surroundings (also known as a wide shot).

Long take
A shot that is held uninterrupted for longer than the conventional duration of a shot, often lasting several minutes.

Master shot
A shot that records an entire scene of dramatic action from start to finish, usually executed as a long shot that keeps all the actors in view.

Match cut
A cut that helps sustain visual and thematic continuity by having characters, objects and/or other compositional elements in one shot match those of the subsequent shot.

Medium shot
A shot executed at a medium distance from the action.

Montage
An editing technique in which short shots are assembled into a rhythmic, time-compressed sequence intended to convey an idea or theme and/or the passage of time.

Moviola
The trademark of an upright machine used to view and edit film.

Negative
The original footage that comes out of the camera and must be processed at a laboratory before a print can be struck from it.

Non-linear editing
A common method of editing that allows random, non-sequential access to the material without destroying it.

180-degree rule
A basic principle of editing that states that two figures in a scene should always have the same left/right relationship to one another.

Optical effects
A laboratory procedure in which shots are modified, using an optical printer, to achieve fades, dissolves and other effects.

Post-production
A part of the filmmaking process that follows principal photography and includes sound and picture editing and addition of visual effects.

Synchronize
To match the picture with the correct sound.

Trim bin
A device in which trimmed footage is hung or clipped while a sequence is being cut.

Up to camera
Editors' jargon for keeping pace with principal photography by cutting a scene together as quickly as the material for the scene is shot.

Workprint
A rough, working version of a film used during the editing process.

Picture Credits

20th Century Fox/American Zoetrope: 96, 97; Universal: 166.

3H Productions/Shochiku Company: 135.

Anonymous Content/Dune Films: 55.

Arena Films/Camera One/France 2 Cinema/Vega Film/Greenpoint Films: 145TR, 145BR.

Bedford Falls/Initial Ent: 49.

Block 2 Pictures/Jet Tone: 126, 127.

Central Motion Pictures: 72.

City Films/Era International: 136, 137.

Columbia: 26, 27, 68, 69, 106, 107, 156, 157, 158, 159; Sony: 70, 71; Tri-Star: 32, 33CL, 33TL.

Danmarks Radio/Nimbus: 80.

Dreamworks: 92, 93, 94.

F Comme Film/Studio Canal/France 2 Cinema: 148, 149.

Focus Features: 50, 51, 52, 53, 64, 65, 74, 75; Studio Canal: 144, 145T, 145B.

Gracie: 42.

Jet Tone: 122, 123, 125.

The Kobal Collection/20th Century Fox: 86R, 150, 151; 20th Century Fox/Hayes, Kerry: 41; 20th Century Fox/Universal: 162; A Band Apart/Miramax: 183T; Anonymous Content/Dune Films: 54; Beijing Film Studios/China Film Corporation/Hero China International/Wide River Investments: 95; Buena Vista/Walt Disney/Large, Chris: 179; CBS-TV: 100; Columbia: 24, 36, 152; Columbia/Block 2/Jet Tone Films/Shya, Wing: 129; Columbia/Sony/Chuen, Chan Kam: 66; Dreamworks: 104, 105TR, 105TL; Dreamworks/James, David: 88, 105B; Dreamworks SKG/Warner Bros: 115; EMI/Columbia/Warners: 44R, 45C, 45; Focus Features/Kuras, Ellen: 82T, 84; Focus Features/Lee, David: 76, 82B, 84; Focus Features/Studio Canal/Ferrandis, Guy: 140; Golden Harvest Group: 132, 133; Independent Pictures: 83; Jet Tone: 120, 124; Les Productions du Trésor/Europa Corp: 147; Live Entertainment: 182R; Lucasfilm/Paramount: 98; MGM: 43, 118, 119L; Miramax/Buena Vista: 182L; Paradis Films: 138; Paramount: 15, 44BL, 44TL, 45B, 87R, 164, 165; Paramount/Vantage: 56; Paramount/Warner Bros/Morton, Merrick: 154L, 154R, 155; Renn Films/A2/RA12: 142, 143; Shadowboxer LLC: 128; Shochiku: 130; Tiger Moth/Miramax/Bray, Phil: 12; Touchstone Pictures/Hamilton, James: 2, 61; Touchstone/Warner Bros/Duhamel, Francois: 169B, 169T; Touchstone/Warner Bros/Vaughan, Stephen: 169C; United Artists: 119R; Universal: 33R, 86L, 102, 103, 183B; Universal/Boland, Jason: 172; Universal/Morton, Merrick: 33BL; Warner Bros: 5, 6, 87L, 87B, 108, 111, 112, 170, 171; Warner Bros/DC Comics: 168; Warner Bros/Marshak, Bob: 46; Zoetrope/United Artists: 34.

Malpaso Productions: 116.

Miramax/Doug Liman: 48.

Murch, Walter, with thanks: 184–185

New Line: 58, 59.

New Regency: 30, 31.

Nimbus Films: 78, 79.

Paramount: 28, 29, 38, 40; Vantage: 62; 63; Warner Bros: 154T, 160;.

Renn/A2/Rai-2: 146.

Shochiku: 139.

Spike Prod/BBC: 90, 91.

Tiger Moth/MiraMax: 22, 23.

United Artists/ Hecht-Hill-Lancaster: 117.

Universal: 174, 175, 176, 178, 180, 181.

Warner Bros: 73, 113, 114; Plan B/Scott Free: 60.

Zoetrope/United Artists: 16, 17, 18, 19, 20, 21.

Index

This book is dedicated to the memory of my father, C.C. Chang, who couldn't have known what he was getting me into when he introduced me to the world of Rosalind Russell and Barbara Stanwyck, Vittorio De Sica and Alfred Hitchcock. Though he didn't live to see its completion, I like to think he would have been pleased by this particular outcome. This is for you, Dad.

Justin Chang